'WHO WERE THE DRUIDS?'

'Who were the Druids?'

*Facts you may have wanted to know,
about the basic themes of early Welsh history*

Michael Senior

First published in 2015

© Text: Michael Senior

ISBN: 978-1-84524-241-1

Published by
Llygad Gwalch,
Ysgubor Plas, Llwyndyrys, Pwllheli, Gwynedd, Wales, LL53 6NG.
Tel: 01758 740432
e-mail: books@carreg-gwalch.com
www.carreg-gwalch.com

Contents

Note: The 'bibliographies' given at the end of each chapter (in place of footnotes) are listed in the order of their relevance to the text.

Introduction

Some of the work involved in writing history consists of checking what the acknowledged experts say; in the process you get to read a lot of books. Only a few times have I been in the position to do original research. Exciting moments those, when you hold in your hands a primary source: the Victorian visitors' books from Snowdon summit, which I tracked down when writing *Yr Wyddfa*; the letter from Alice Hargreaves (as Alice in Wonderland became) regarding Lewis Carroll's possible visit to Llandudno, which was made available to me in the library at Christ Church college, Oxford.

Usually all the books one checks sing the same song, but I always bear in mind that this might be for a wrong reason. These learned people have not usually been able to do original research either, but they trust each other. Thus if one of them at some point took a wrong direction they would all set off along that path. Something, in the process, becomes assumed to be fact, even if it is wrong. Consequently if somebody at any stage expresses a different opinion to the conventional wisdom it is worth taking it seriously.

I know that mistakes can be made, even by eminent academics. What most people do not fully realise is that such an error can get passed from one expert to another until it quite changes its nature. So it is viewed as an established fact, perhaps, that William Wordsworth came to Conwy, although he doesn't anywhere say that he did. It is an established fact that Edward I presented his infant son to the people of Wales as their Prince, although the boy only became Prince of Wales some decades later. It is usually given as an established fact that Queen Eleanor grew flowers on the barbican of Conwy castle, in spite of the fact that she only went there once and very briefly.

This book tries to redress the balance by referring in each case to the evidence, scant though it might sometimes be. It is what I did in the case of Gelert, of Beddgelert fame, of Lewis Carroll in relation to his disputed visit to Llandudno, and of Prince Madoc's famous voyage to America. I recognise that I have to accept that not everybody will believe me, casting well-authenticated doubt on some cherished assumptions, since in the end people undoubtedly prefer fiction to fact.

1

Celt and Saxon

In the seventh century BC two groups of people faced each other across the river Rhine. One group had originally occupied the more habitable parts of southern Scandinavia, where they had remained for a long time unchallenged. By the seventh century however their success there had led to population growth, with the inevitable results of expansion, competition, conflict. The other had originated in two separate groups based on an area of what is now Austria, stretching along the northern edge of the Alps as far as eastern France, and their culture was carried into many parts of Europe during the first millennium BC.

Although (as we shall see) these people were subsequently known by several names, they are as near as we can get to identifying the origins of the Saxons and the Celts.

When they met on the Rhine there was no great distinction between them other than that of language. In fact they began straight away to merge, so that right from the start we have no easy way, apart from language, of distinguishing between the Saxons and the Celts. As Christopher Hawkes puts it, in his seminal work on Iron Age hill-forts: "a mingling of Celtic and Germanic features soon begins to be perceptible in archaeology of that region". This "mixed Celto-Germanic culture was destined to persist there for many centuries" and in due course formed the background to the later invaders of Britain known as the

Belgae. These Belgic invaders were thus "of mixed Celtic and Germanic stock", and it is they who formed the population of southern Britain when the Romans came.

Archaeologically the one group, representing the ancestors of the Celts, were distinguished by such things as a short sword, with a horseshoe-shaped pommel, and by the custom of cremation. These styles identified the first group of them investigated, at Hallstatt, a village in Austria, in a series of digs between 1846 and 1862. Some variations were revealed by discoveries made at La Tène, at the east end of Lake Neuchatel in Switzerland, in 1858. It could be argued (and so of course sometimes is) that the slight variations between the Hallstatt and the La Tène cultures meant that the people who came to be known to antiquarians as 'Celtic' were not one cultural group but two, and indeed when they both reached Britain they are known to archaeologists by the even more impersonal names of Iron Age A and Iron Age B.

The other major group converging at this time, known to the Romans eventually as *Teutones* or *Germani* were also distinguished by a type of weapon, in their case again a kind of knife or single-edged sword, known to them as *seax*, from which they may have gained their identifying name of Saxons.

They were not culturally distinct, then, when we first get to know about them through their artefacts. Moreover it had never been the case that either were a distinct ethnic group. This is only partly for the obvious reason that they are both groups of white Europeans from the temperate zone. Research, following the mapping of the human genome, has recently concluded that genetic variations occur as much within as between apparent ethnic groups.

Our next step in getting to know about them turns from

the examination of their remains to the notes that were made about them, albeit by their enemies. First, though, we should examine how they came to be known by the names we use for them.

Herodotus, Greek historian of the fifth century BC, took from a slightly earlier historian Hecateus the name *Keltoi* to refer to the barbarian (i.e. non-Greek) people of the European continent in general, mentioning their connection with the area of the source of the Danube in particular. Posidonius, whose work comes to us through slightly later Greek authors, Diodurus Siculus and Strabo, evidently knew some more about this – and he is important to us as an influence on Caesar. Caesar says, evidently from this source,

Julius Caesar Statue in Louvre Museum, Paris

that *Celtae* was what they called themselves. He however knew them as *Galli*.

Professor Kenneth Jackson told Stuart Piggot in the 1960s that all this is linguistic nonsense. The word 'Celt' is probably a corruption of the Greek *Galatoi*; but this did not prevent its becoming embedded in the writings of early historians, and the fact of its having been used in the first sentence of *De Bello Gallico* was enough to ensure its survival. The Gauls were Celts – whether supposedly a part of a larger group going by that name, or co-extensive with them, is not quite clear.

Caesar, in *De Bello Gallic*, describes the customs of the 'Gauls' and the 'Germans' as being different, yet both in his account are warlike and capable of savagery, a trait of the Gauls which is corroborated by the earlier Greek historian Strabo: "The whole race... is madly fond of war." Unfortunately Caesar does not tell us what the two groups looked like. More than a hundred years later Tacitus enlarged on Caesar's records, drawing from other contemporary sources. From the two accounts we get a close look at what at least the Roman authors thought was the difference between the Germans and the Gauls. The first visible sight we get of any of them is after the Roman invasion of Britain. Since Tacitus tells us that the Caledonians appeared to be of German origin because they had reddish hair and large limbs, we know at least what he thought that Germans were like. Blue eyes (he confirms in *Germania*), reddish hair and huge frames. When he says that the people who lived nearest to the Gauls looked like them, we know only that they were probably not dark and curly-haired like the Silures, since these characteristics led him to think that the latter came from Spain.

The name of the other group, 'Saxons', seems possibly to have come about by accident. When Ptolomy, the Greek geographer, wrote his *Geographia* in the second century AD, he mentioned a tribe which he called *Saxones* as living north of the river Elbe. There is apparently some textual uncertainty here, since some copies of his work call them *Axones* and Tacitus in the *Germania* names apparently the

Tacitus

same tribe *Aviones*. The loss of the first letter, however, is explained by some scholars as scribal error, and the most uncontentious view seems to be that it is right to say that Ptolomy used the word *Saxones*, and that he was the first to do so. By the time the Romans had come to Britain the term was in common use to describe the people of northern Europe. The Emperor Julian mentioned them in the 4th century as supporters of a rival emperor, and the Romans called their series of forts along the English Channel coastlines the *Litus Saxonicum*, the Saxon coast.

Named by us now as a hybrid entity, the mixed group which became known as the Anglo-Saxons are usually known to their enemies by one half of that name, and to themselves by the other. The *Sais* or *Sassenach* speak a language called *Saesneg*, but we hear more about the other group, who identify themselves by the Latin term *Angli* and refer to their king as *Rex Anglorum*. As a linguistic term Anglo-Saxon perhaps has retrospective meaning, since eventually the Saxon and Anglian languages merged, to give us English. They themselves (from Alfred onwards) called their tongue *Anglisc*, though the former inhabitants of the island continued to regard them and their language as Saxon, as indeed they still do.

Though still calling them Gauls and Germans both Caesar and Tacitus are detailed in their descriptions of the customs and characteristics of the people who became known to us as the Celts and Saxons. Caesar sees the Gauls as being extremely superstitious and practising an organised religion. He sees the Druids as being the most important class, closely followed by the 'Knights'. Druids officiate at worship and hand down religious and civil judgements. They teach the doctrine of re-incarnation and study astronomy. He gives a list of the gods they worship, using the Roman equivalent: Mercury first, then Apollo, Mars, Jupiter and Minerva. "The customs of the Germans are entirely different." They have no Druids to control religious observance, and are not much given to sacrifices. They have, says Caesar, no abstract deities, worshipping only gods they can see: Sun, Moon, and Fire. "The other gods they have never heard of."

Here then, we may feel, lies a fundamental difference: the Germans are not said to have had a priesthood, whereas the Gauls are seen as being ruled by one. Germans are perhaps solely militaristic, Gauls more contemplative? The only trouble with this neat dichotomy is that it is then contradicted by Tacitus. Tacitus tells us that the Germans believed in a founding deity and a god of battle, indicating at least some religious observance. They evidently had sacred groves, which is what other classical authors associated with the Druids. "They also carry into the fray figures and emblems from their sacred groves." "Above all gods they worship Mercury", which is exactly what Caesar told us of the Gauls. After Mercury comes Hercules, and (like the Gauls) Mars. "Some of the Suebi sacrifice to Isis also." Their holy places are not temples but 'woods and groves'. In fact, just like the Druids, as Tacitus himself describes elsewhere. Moreover, far from worshipping only gods that they can see "they call by the name of god that hidden presence which is seen by the eye of reverence." Their priests, he tells us, preside over their assemblies, just as Caesar has told us that the Druids did in the customs of the Gauls. The Germans, as Tacitus sees them, were obsessed with portents (echoing Caesar's description of the Gauls as highly superstitious). They also take gambling (with dice) extremely seriously.

There is another curious anomaly between the two historians which makes one wonder whether there has perhaps been some textual confusion. Caesar of the Gauls, and Tacitus of the Germans, mentions a social habit evidently unusual to the Romans, and in almost exactly the same words. It is the respective group's method of measuring time. Caesar says of the Gauls "..they measure period of time not by days but by nights", and Tacitus of the Germans: "They count, not like us, by days, but by nights." (N) Whatever the explanation of this duplication, it at least adds no support to the idea that the customs of the Germans are entirely different to those of the Gauls.

It is agreed that both groups were warlike, though we might feel that this was an unsurprising response to the approach of the might of Rome. The Gauls were seen by both historians as being decadent as a result of living near the

Roman province, giving a militant advantage to the Germans. Tacitus on the other hand, while agreeing with this assessment, sees the Germans as lazy, getting up late, spending their time more in idling, sleep and gluttony, than in war or hunting. Their drinking bouts lasted a day and a night and often ended in fights. This accusation of idleness, binge-drinking and yob culture hardly supports a distinction between the groups based on the theory that the Gauls were decadent.

Some such contrast as indicated by Caesar and Tacitus has, however, become traditional. Wade-Evans, writing in the 1930s, traces the origins of our recent stereotype to Captain David Jones's 1706 translation of the Abbé Pezron's book *Antiquité de la Nation et de la langue des Celtes*,

"wherein the 'Celtae or Gauls' are 'our ancient Britains' (sic) etc.". The seed, he says, sprouted and flourished, until Ernest Renan's *Essai sur la Poesie des Races Celtique*, of 1854, inspired Matthew Arnold to write his 'Essay on Celtic Literature', in 1867. This was the culmination of a programme of Arnold's to promote the idea of a Celtic cultural world, and it is a sort of summary of his 'Lectures on Celtic Literature' which he delivered at Oxford in the years 1865 and 6. In these he put forward three themes which he saw as identifyingly Celtic:

Matthew Arnold

'Celtic Magic', 'Celtic Melancholy', and the predominance of style over structure. "These works", says Wade-Evans, are "full of delightful nonsense". Certainly the wild generalisations of the Arnold polemics seem laughable to us now, but the fact is that it was his influence, as much as anyone's, which set the thinking which still bedevils the subject – that is, that the Welsh, Scottish and Irish are Celtic, and that this makes them different.

Ironically Arnold is often accused of a fault of which he was not guilty, that of dismissing as irrelevant and harmful the Welsh language, which were in fact the views expressed by a leader in The Times following the publication of an open letter from Arnold to a Welsh colleague, Hugh Owen, in which he says that "to preserve and honour the Welsh language and literature is quite compatible with not thwarting or delaying for a single hour the introduction, so undeniably useful, of a knowledge of English among all classes in Wales." The Times leader (of September 1866) was more intolerant on the subject. The Welsh language was "the curse of Wales" and responsible for excluding the Welsh people "from the civilisation, the improvement, and the material prosperity of their English neighbours". There were some villages, it said with horror, where "not more than two or three persons" habitually spoke English. "...this persistent prevalence of the Welsh language is one of the greatest misfortunes of their countrymen." "Their antiquated and semibarbarous language shrouds them in darkness." Worthwhile achievements in Europe "have come mainly from Teutonic sources" and "The sooner all Welsh specialities disappear from the face of the earth the better." Arnold, it says, had become "more Welsh than the Welsh", a sentimentalist guilty of "arrant nonsense".

Hardly surprisingly Matthew Arnold took the first opportunity to reply, using the Introduction of the publication in book form of his Celtic Literature lectures, in 1867, to berate The Times and put forward (quoting his letter to Owen) what was clearly his considered opinion on the matter of Celticness. Celticness shines in contrast to the 'Philistinism' of the English middle class. 'Vulgarity', 'coarseness', 'unintelligence' were their defining qualities. "Now, then, is the moment for the greater delicacy and spirituality of the Celtic peoples who are blended with us, if it be but wisely directed, to make itself prized and honoured."

If we turn now from the written to the material evidence, there is, as before, no immediate sign of one cultural group living up to this ideal by being more refined or sophisticated than the other.

Celtic work is notably curvilinear, a form which favours intertwined and labyrinthine patterns. But that is also exactly what we find on brooches from the continental homelands of the Saxons and related work in Saxon areas of Britain, such as may be seen in Norwich Castle museum and in the Ashmolean in Oxford. A great gold buckle found at the burial site of Sutton Hoo, now in the British Museum, is of mesmerising curvilinear, intertwined complexity. It is, we begin to feel, only their languages that can tell them apart.

We do not have written material from the two peoples themselves before they entered Britain. Caesar tells us that the Gauls could write, and he says in fact that they used the Greek alphabet. The only reason they left no records, it seems, is that the Druids forbade it. Their reliance on oral memorising was to some extent more of a safeguard of tradition than written matter would have been; and it is certainly possible that what was handed down orally in

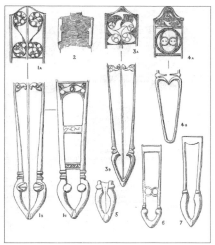

Celtic art on hilted daggers 75-40 BC

classical times eventually got incorporated into the literature. We do not hear whether the Germans at this stage could write or not.

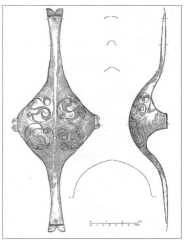

*Celtic art on shield bosses,
Llyn Cerrig Bach (Anglesey)*

Two very early works of literature, one for each side, belonging to the period after the invasions, deal with a memory of the distant origins of their people and so throw some light on what they thought their ancestors had been like. In the one case *Beowulf* belongs (at least in intention) to the first part of the 6th century, and in the other, *Y Gododdin*, towards the end of that same century – though both works of course come to us in later forms. Both relate to a time which the writers saw as being of ancestral purity, and so they are the nearest we are likely to get to the mindset of the original people. The Gododdin depicts what one of its editors has called "the life of a warlike society governed by martial ideals and heroic concepts of behaviour". The blood-thirsty attitude of the participants is amply illustrated. For instance:

Goreu hwn cyn cystlwn cerennydd
Ennaint crau ac angau o'i hennydd

(1.111-112) 'He made, sooner than speak of peace,/ a blood-bath and death for his adversary.'

And

Oedd garw y gwnaewch chwi waedlin,
Mal y fed medd trwy chwerthin:

(1.674-5) 'Fiercely did you make blood flow/ Like drinking mead while laughing.'

In fact this is as far as one could get from the "sensibility and nervous exaltation", the "delicate magic" of which "Celtic romance is so pre-eminently a mistress", which for Matthew Arnold give rise to Celtic Magic.

Beowulf was written down later, perhaps about the year 1000, and according to one recent study composed in East Anglia, but it harks back to a time before the ancestors of its contemporaries left their homelands. The original settlers, we are told, had no written tradition. As Kevin Crossley - Holland puts it in his book *The Anglo-Saxon World*: "Their history and legends were transmitted only by word of mouth in the form of lays – compressed narrative poems – and comprised a common Germanic inheritance..." The story is centred on a drinking-hall, clearly an important focus of the tradition.

Him on mod bearn
Thaet healreced hatan wolde,
Medoaern micel men gewyrcean.

(1.67-9) 'It came to mind that he would instruct men to build a greater mead-hall than the children of men had ever heard of...'

The enemy threatening the comfort of the people of *Beowulf* is not a rival nation, but a counterpart world, a world of supernatural fantasy, giving rise to a mood of literature which is distinctly other-worldly, constantly expressing a wishful reaching-out into the unknown, the non-human. The ethos of *Beowulf* in fact comes nearer to what Tacitus described as "that hidden presence which is seen by the eye of reverence". Anglo-Saxon poetry in general is described as elegiac – Crossley-Holland, for instance: "It has been said that in Anglo-Saxon poetry, the lyric mood is always elegiac." Often the poet's song is of loss: "it is mournful and plangent". It cannot but strike us that although this is the sort of thing the Victorians said about the literature of the 'Celts', it is a long way from the often brutal realism rooted in a relish of the hard ferocity of a defensive way of life which characterises *Y Gododdin*.

One area in which a certain difference between the groups is apparent was hinted at by Caesar and only first revealed itself in an early form after the coming of Christianity to

St Columba

Iona

Britain. Caesar said of the social structure of the Gauls that division of the tribe into groups was an ancient custom, which he saw as a desire "to ensure that all common people should have protection against the strong: for each leader sees that no one get the better of his supporters by force or by cunning...." It is perhaps with hindsight that we can say that here we catch a glimpse of a society in which immediate power is widely disseminated and counterbalanced.

When Christianity came to Britain it came at two different times and from two different directions. It is no surprise to find that it came also in two different styles, which we may conveniently call the Celtic and the Anglian. The Celtic version came with missionaries from the great monasteries of Ireland, notably St Columba who came to Iona (off the isle of Mull) from Ireland in 563. Iona became the base for British Christianity and a paradigm of the monastic system. Christianity was even then by no means new in Britain; the evangelical pioneering saints had been at work since the time of Pelagius, who went from Britain to Rome in the late 4th century. Pelagius held, contrary to the orthodox dogma exemplified by the works of St Augustine of Hippo, that personal will and responsibility were superior in the matter of belief to centralised hierarchic authority. We are free to use our own efforts to achieve our own salvation. The point about introducing this subject here is that Augustine's followers accused Pelagius of trying to bring back Druidism, and indeed it seems likely that the social attitudes which had at one time favoured Druidism inspired Pelagius too. By the time the great wave of belief arrived via Iona a distinctly British (and therefore 'Celtic') attitude to religion had become established in this country. Community-based, not reliant on a superior authority, we may see in it the seeds of

St Augustine

an egalitarian society to be served in due course by a non-conformist church, in which the minister is not imposed by, or beholden to, a distant power, but can be sacked by his congregation if he fails to please them.

This is in stark contrast to the situation set up by another St Augustine's mission to Kent. He came on the express orders of Pope Gregory I, with a large retinue of clergy and interpreters, in the year 595. Augustine was a monk in Rome, prior of St Andrew's monastery, but he became a bishop before he reached Britain on his way to a mission to the colonists in Kent. Right from the start he sent messengers back to Rome for instructions on the conduct of the mission, and then on the details of church life and church politics. Pope Gregory in due course demanded, over all that distance, that the Christians of Wales and Cornwall should submit to Augustine's authority. A meeting between the two branches of Christianity in Britain ended in failure. Gregory continued to transmit laws and instructions to the new religious colony in Kent, which was explicitly accountable to him as Pope – but he clearly had no influence over the 'Celtic' branch of the same religion.

It may be beginning to become obvious to us that although there is no material difference between the two groups of

Canterbury Cathedral

people we summarise as the Celts and the Saxons, there is a subtle inbuilt difference of attitude. It also remains the fact that their languages came from different branches of the overall Indo-European family.

The early languages of Britain, which have survived to varying extents in present-day variations – Welsh, Irish and Scottish Gaelic, Cornish and Manx – have sufficient elements in common to point to the assumption of a common original. There are traces indicating this ancestor all over Europe, and as long ago as the 16th century George Buchanan, a Scottish humanist, proposed grouping the modern descendants of this into a family of languages, which he termed 'Celtic', as in the Celtic branch, like the Latin branch and the Germanic branch, of the Indo-European group of languages. We have seen that there was no real justification for the choice of term, since Celtic was, in the minds of Roman historians, the description of one group of the peoples of Europe in ancient times. Buchanan's work was pursued by Edward Lhuyd, scientist (botanist and chemist, later philologist), who became Keeper of the recently-founded Ashmolean Museum at Oxford, at the start of the 18th century, and from his classification it became clear that the close correlation does indeed form them into a language group. It is now accepted that these 'Celtic' languages have derived from the assumed original mother-language known as Indo-European, which is regarded as having been spoken by a nomadic people living on the steppes of western Central Asia from about 4000 BC, from where they migrated into India, the Middle East and Europe, where the language began to diversify into its modern daughter languages as different groups lost contact with one another. The Celtic sub-group then developed, very widely spread, along with the 'Hallstatt' culture with which it is associated, and the ornamental metalwork which also identifies that culture. As the languages developed they formed themselves into two branches, the 'P' and the Q', just as did the Latin sub-group (for instance) and its modern derivatives, where Latin itself is a 'Q'-branch language, and Greek a 'P' one. This is well exemplified in the word for five, *quinque* in Latin, *pente* in Greek.

So into the P group fall Brythonic (British Celtic, now best represented by Welsh), Gaulish, and Ligurian – the Celtic language of northern Italy; and those spoken in central Europe and in Anatolia. Into the Q group went other variants spoken in Iberia, and the Gaelic language of Ireland. In Welsh the word for five is *pump*, and in old Irish

Gaelic it is *coic*, now *a cuig*, (where the c has developed from q).

Turning now to the languages spoken by the Angles and the Saxons, these technically belong to the Germanic group, originating it is thought in the first millennium BC as something now known as Proto-Germanic, a branch of Indo-European which is conventionally broken up into three sub-groups, East, North, and West Germanic. The last of these is further divided into Continental and North-Sea Germanic, and among the second sub-group ('North-Sea Germanic') are to be found Anglo-Frisian and Old Saxon.

Of course this is an exercise in taxonomy rather than analysis, since the remaining evidence for the existence of these earlier languages is small, consisting of a few runic inscriptions, some of which are illegible. Language derivation is inevitably to some extent argued backwards from the characteristics of present-day 'daughter' languages to an ultimately hypothetical common original. But it can be indicated with some confidence that Frisian split off from its Anglic association through becoming increasingly influenced by Dutch and Low German, while Anglic was influenced by Norse and by non-Germanic languages such as French. Saxon in the meantime (the original version of which is called Old Saxon) is a sub-branch of Low Germanic, itself a division of Continental West German, which happened to end up side-by-side with its North-Sea Germanic counterpart Anglic, to form what one authority has called a linguistic crossroads, and give rise to our notion of Anglo-Saxon.

We shall have reason to consider the origins of the people who spoke these two dialects of Old Germanic when we observe them in a later chapter as they enter our island. It is clear that they were not a single self-identifying group.

Similarly the 'Celts' whom they found there had combined into a cohesive group gradually and relatively recently, from what is now thought of as "a major group of people in Iron Age Europe who spoke closely related languages and who shared much the same religious beliefs, art styles, fashions in dress and weapons, social structure and values". Or, taking a different, perhaps more realistic view, "a large number of ethnic groups who occupied much of central and western Europe in the first millennium BC and spoke a series of related dialects which linguists define as 'Celtic'".

Bibliography

George Kraft. 'The Origin of the Kelts'. *Antiquity*, Vol. III. No. 9. March, 1929. Trs. Professor V. Gordon Childe.

Christopher Hawkes. 'Hill-Forts'. *Antiquity*, Vol. V. No. 17 pp. 62, 89.

Report of Howard University, Washington D.C. *The Times*, 27th October, 2004. p. 16.

Stuart Piggott. *Celts, Saxons and the Early Antiquaries*. The O'Donnell Lecture 1966. Edinburgh University Press, 1967. For an interesting discussion of the trend of modern terminology to move from 'Gauls' to 'Celts' see Jonathan Williams, *Beyond the Rubicon: Romans and Gauls in Republican Italy*. Oxford, 2001.

Strabo iv. iv. 2. cited in Colin Renfrew, *Archaeology and Language*. Jonathan Cape, 1987.

Tacitus. *On Britain and Germany*. Trs. H. Mattingley. Penguin Books, 1948.

Julius Caesar. *The Conquest of Gaul*. Trs. S. A. Handforth. Penguin Books, 1951.

A. W. Wade-Evans. *Welsh Christian Origins*. The Alden Press, Oxford, 1934.

James Campbell (ed.) *The Anglo-Saxons*. Book Club Associates, 1982.

A. O. H. Jarman (ed.) *Y Gododdin*. Gomer Press. 1990.

Kevin Crossley-Holland. *The Anglo-Saxon World*. Boydell Press, 1982.

Archaeologia Britannica, 1707.

John Haywood. *The Celts. Bronze Age to New Age*. Longmans, 2004.

Barry Cunliffe. *The Ancient Celts*. Oxford University Press, 1997.

N: In fact the transferred passage from Caesar's text has been explained to me by Professor Rhiannon Ash, (Fellow of Merton College, Oxford, lecturer in Classics and a modern authority on Tacitus), as resulting from the expanding borders of the Empire. When Caesar was writing the Gauls "retained a certain mystique", but were too well-known by the time of Tacitus to be found strange, "so many of the peculiar ethnographical details of Caesar's text were appropriately shifted to the Germans beyond the Rhine, still a suitably mysterious group".

2

The Druids

There is abundant material by Greek and Roman historians on the subject of the Druids, but only a little of this dates from the period when they were said to exist, and some of that slight evidence is, we shall see, probably copied from or influenced by the rest of it. Much of the testimony is thus about the past, and so assumedly elaborated by hearsay. All of it is biased, a form of propaganda, seeking to promote the popular idea that the early tribes of Europe were quaint and irrational in their behaviour compared to Roman civilisation. The purpose of this was to justify the expansion of the empire into central and western Europe. We were doing them a favour, it implied, by stamping out barbaric customs and ignorance, implanting a less primitive attitude and a belief in more sensible gods. But this evidence is all we have.

There is no other contemporary evidence for the existence of the Druids. They did not leave any record of themselves, since although they were able to write they chose not to; nor did they have any historians of their nations who might have left for us a view of the other side of the story. There are no material items which can be identified as associated with them – no archaeological finds which attest to their activities, no legacy of their lives.

Of the four classical writers alive at the time of the Roman invasion of Gaul who mention the Druids only one, Posidonius (or Poseidonius), could claim to be a first-hand witness, and his texts are lost. They are only known to us from references and quotation in the work of others. Of the other three (Diodorus Siculus, Julius Caesar, and Strabo) all are influenced both by Posidonius and by each other. They thus fail to stand as reliable independent witnesses.

Posidonius

Posidonius was a Greek born in northern Syria and educated in Athens in the Stoic tradition, who later became a follower of the school of Aristotle. He lived from about 135 to about 51 BC. In about 95 BC he moved to Rhodes, which he made his home. Through an involvement with politics he was able to travel widely throughout the Roman empire. One of these journeys took him to Gaul, probably at a time shortly before its invasion by Caesar. Wherever he went he made detailed notes of what he saw in a spirit which we now recognise as scientific. In Cadiz at the far end of Spain he noted the tides' connection wth the phases of the moon. In Alexandria he used the position of a star to calculate the circumference of the Earth. In Gaul he studied the Celts, and wrote a paper on them. We do not have the text, since as mentioned the works of Posidonius only exist for us now as fragments mined from references in the works of others, but we do know quite a lot about what he said, because it is (sometimes explicitly) cited in the writings of Timagenes, Strabo, Diodorus Siculus, Caesar and Tacitus.

Strabo is one of our best sources. He lived between 64 BC

Strabo

and 24 AD, and so was writing at what he saw as the end of a period, about how things used to be. Of the Gauls he said "at the present time they are all at peace, ... but it is from the early times that I am taking this account of them", perhaps acknowledging his source as Posidonius. He says of the Druids, for instance, that "in former times they .. arbitrated cases of war..." A Greek born in what is now Turkey in an area which had by then become Roman, he studied under the grammarian Aristodemus, who was the grandson of Posidonius, – and probably this connection had an influence on his choice of evidence which shows up in his work. Like other Romanised Greeks of his period he used his position as a supporter of the empire to travel widely within it, in the newly safer world of Roman rule. It was the reign of Augustus, and what must have seemed like the whole world was basking in the *pax romana*.

Strabo wrote about his travels in the form of a great continuing work, his 'Geographica'. The other notable work by him was his Historical Sketches, which is referred to by other authors and of which only a fragment remains. The Geographica however was widely copied and is available to us in what we have every reason to suppose is a true form.

Strabo identifies three respected classes of distinction among the Gauls, evidently separate from the fighting men and military leaders, and evidently, since he finds them worth mentioning, unfamiliar to the Romans. They were the bards, for which he uses the Greek word *Bardoi*, described as singers and poets; the prophets (*ovateis*), "diviners and natural philosophers"; and the Druids, *druidai*, who studied moral as well as natural philosophy. "The Druids are considered the most just of men, and on this account they are entrusted with the decision, not only of the private disputes, but of public disputes as well." They formed, in other words, a sort of court of law, but with philosophical overtones. Some religious belief (but at this stage no mention of ritual) is also implied. Not only the Druids, says Strabo, but people in general, consider that human souls and the universe itself are indestructible.

The Druids are thus considered a source of wisdom and regulators of justice, and these functions are borne out (perhaps not surprisingly) by a source perhaps even closer to the original remarks of Posidonius, Diodorus Siculus, a Greek historian from Sicily, who wrote between the years 60 and 30 BC. He produced a vast work of historical and geographic study, which he called Biblioteca historica, a history library, indicating that he saw it as a

Diodorus

collection rather than a creation. Some of its forty books are lost, but we have copies of some fourteen books. Diodorus gives the same three categories of wise men among the Gauls: "There are among them lyric poets, whom they call Bards...

Philosophers, as we may call them, and men learned in religious affairs, are unusually honoured among them and are called by them Druids. The Gauls likewise make use of diviners, accounting them worthy of high approbation..." Both these authors then give an account of the practice of human sacrifice by the Gauls, but this is not said by them to have been carried out by the Druids. Indeed Strabo implies that the Druids were some sort of moderating power in such practices: "But they would not sacrifice without the Druids". He is, at this point, explicitly quoting Posidonius, quoting him as saying (of other barbarous customs) "he himself saw this spectacle in many places". Diodorus says that "it is a custom of theirs that no one should perform a sacrifice without a 'philosopher' ", by which he almost certainly means a Druid, since he has said, above, that the Druids were "Philosophers, as we may call them...."

These are the main conveyors of the possibly first-hand reports of Posidonius; there are hints, but no certainty, that there might have been more information, which we have not got. Timagenes, for instance, who wrote his 'History of the Kings' not long after 55 BC, in Rome, and whose works are lost (because he himself destroyed them), is referred to with respect by Diodorus Siculus, and cited as authoritative by Amminianus in the 4th century AD. It is possible that information was available to Timagenes (who made a special study of the Gauls) additional to that which was preserved from Posidonius, but we cannot be sure and anyway it seems as if it would support the little knowledge which we have – which is, roughly, that Gaulish society had three classes of intellectuals of which the Druids were one. It is only when we come to the slightly later Roman writers such as Caesar, Tacitus and Pliny, that we get any further insight into what (at least) the Roman writers thought that the Druids were and did. It is ironic, but perhaps typical, that the further we get from the time when the Druids were supposed to have flourished the more information about them becomes available.

Both Pliny and Tacitus were writing in the first century AD, but Caesar wrote in about 52 BC, and he was in Gaul off and on between 58 and 50, so he was present in the immediate aftermath of the Celtic world which he describes from past reports, and which he himself helped to destroy. There are portions of *De Bello Gallico* which are recognisably interpolations, added by copiers at a later date, and parts of it where Caesar is currently held to be unreliable, so that although we have much information from his book we do not know how much of it to trust. I will not deal in detail with these textual problems here, partly because I am not qualified to do so, partly because I imagine the readers to consider other aspects of the matter to be of more interest. We will now see, however, the route by which the Druids acquired their present image.

Caesar writes with confident authority that there were two classes held in high respect in Gaul, not, as his near-contemporaries have said, three, and he does not include like them bards and prophets. He said that in the part of Gaul he was writing about these were the Druids and the *equites* – horsemen, usually translated as Knights. The Druids he portrays as priests – they officiated at religious services, and ruled on doctrinal questions. They formed an educational institution: 'large numbers of young men came to them for instruction'. Caesar gives them a much wider sphere of activity than the other authors: they were lawyers, judges and politicians, settling both personal disputes and tribal conflicts. The penalty for not obeying them was excommunication: being 'banned from taking part in sacrifice – the heaviest punishment that can be inflicted upon a Gaul'. The Druids were ruled by a chief, who governed for life, his successor being chosen (if there is more than one candidate) by vote, or occasionally by conflict. Once a year the Druids meet at a sacred place in the centre of Gaul.

Then he actually mentions Britain. The Druidic doctrine is thought to have been invented (*reperta*) in Britain, and to have been imported into Gaul from there, and 'even today' people who want to study it in depth usually go to Britain to do so.

Caesar fills out the role and functions of the Druids in some detail. They are exempt from taxes and from military service. But joining their ranks is no easy option. It can take twenty years of study to qualify, because you have to learn by heart a great number of verses. It has to be all memorised because there is a prohibition on writing:

> The Druids believe that their religion forbids them to commit their teachings to writing, although for most other purposes, such as public and private accounts, the Gauls use the Greek alphabet.

Caesar analyses this proscription. He imagines, he says, that the rule was originally established because they did not want their doctrine to become public property. It also had the benefit of training the memories of their pupils rather than relying on the written word. It is an interesting consideration that it might well be because of this rule that the Gauls kept no written records, and as a result we have no sight of the scene in Europe at this time from their point of view, and also, rather tragically, have lost much of the wisdom which had been accumulated by the Druids over presumably a long period.

Caesar does however preserve a little of this for us. They taught that the soul is indestructible and passes at death from one person to another – in other words the belief in reincarnation and transmigration of souls associated with the Greek school of Pythagoras. This doctrine, for the Gauls, mitigated the loss of death. They also taught (he says) what we would now call cosmology, the size, makeup and behaviour of the earth and the universe. Almost in passing he mentions the wicker man, and this custom is only indirectly related to the Druids. When in battle the Gauls might offer to the gods, or vow to offer, human sacrifice, 'for the performance of which they employ Druids'. They have regular state ceremonies of such sacrifices. "Some tribes have colossal images made of wickerwork, the limbs of which

Caesar's mention of the 'wicker man' caught the imagination of early illustrators

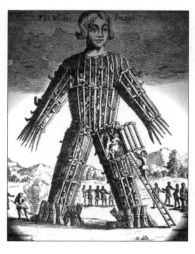

they fill with living men; they are then set on fire, and the victims burnt to death." It is clear that Caesar regards the Druids as exclusively a Gaulish institution. He says explicitly of the Germans that "they have no Druids".

Professor Ronald Hutton, whom I think might be regarded as an up-to-date authority on this subject, has some qualifications to make about Caesar's account. In his work *The Pagan Religions of the Ancient British Isles*, for instance, he says that Caesar "had a powerful motive for disparaging" the Gauls "in order to justify his aggressive warfare against them". However Hutton recognises Caesar's ambivalent attitude towards his enemies, and elsewhere in the same book he finds this also biased: "..he had a vested interest in exaggerating the sophistication of the Gallic peoples to the Roman Senate, to support his assertions that they were a good prize if conquered and a threat if not." But if the contention is that Caesar had compelling motives for arguing both ways – the Gauls were barbarians, and the Gauls were sophisticated – then would it not be easier to imagine that he might have told things just as he saw them to be?

Nora Chadwick, one of the most stringent scholars on the subject, says that the Classical writers in general were drawn to "the bizarre, the picturesque, and the curious aspects of druidism" presumably to highlight the civilised nature of the Greek and Roman empires by contrast with the supposedly barbaric customs of the unoccupied lands. "One is conscious throughout their reports that the druids were looked upon as objects of curiosity, rather than of serious interest and dignity in their own right." Pliny presents us with a good example of Chadwick's point.

'Pliny the Elder' (to distinguish him from his nephew,

Pliny the Elder

more famous partly for having recorded the eruption of Vesuvius, in which catastrophe the older Pliny died), was born in the town of Como in 23 AD and started his career as a lawyer. Remaining unmarried and so with no children he eventually adopted his nephew as his heir. The elder Pliny became a prodigious writer, producing a 'History of the German Wars' which, though now lost, formed important source material for Tacitus' Annals and *Germania*. He also had a public life of some distinction. When he died on the shore of the Bay of Naples he was fleet commander of the Roman navy, appointed to that post by the Emperor Vespasian. In that capacity he was stationed at Misenum, across the Bay, when Vesuvius erupted. A message from a friend asking for rescue made him leave the fleet in a faster boat and reach the shore below Pompeii under a deluge of falling pumice. An onshore wind then prevented him from leaving. He became (for some reason) physically unable to move, possibly because of being overweight and asthmatic, and he was left behind while the friends he had come to rescue retreated.

Pliny's account of the druids is elaborate and fanciful, and perhaps because it is likely to be fictional it has become greatly preferred to the mundane and meagre facts. "This picturesque fantasia", says Nora Chadwick, "is almost the

Pliny's fanciful description of Druid rituals is the form best known to us through its influence on Romantic art

only account of the druids that is at all widely known today." She compares it to the stories of King Alfred and the cakes, Cnut and the waves, Bruce and the spider. We shall see shortly the route by which it has entered our cultural consciousness. This is what Pliny actually tells us, in his 'Natural History':

The mistletoe is specially venerated by the Gauls. "The Druids – for that is the name they give to their magicians – hold nothing more sacred than the misletoe and the tree that bears it, supposing always that tree to be the oak (*robur*)." They have groves of oak, where their ceremonies take place, all of which involve the use of branches of oak. The name of this priesthood probably derives from the Greek word for the oak tree. (N1)

Although it is unusual for the mistletoe to be found on the oak, when it does grow there it is gathered by the Druids with religious awe. Pliny then describes the ceremony, which takes place on the fifth day of the moon, the day they start their months and years "because the moon by then has considerable power and influence".

They have a banquet under the trees and sacrifice there two white bulls. "Clad in a white robe the priest ascends the tree, and cuts the mistletoe with a golden sickle, which is received by others in a white cloak." They believe the mistletoe taken as a drink brings fertility to barren animals, and is an antidote to poisons. "Such are the religious feelings which we find entertained towards trifling objects among nearly all nations." Pliny is particularly interested in medicine, and his Natural History keeps reverting to it.

A little later he tells the remarkable story of the Serpent's egg, which he says, probably correctly, has been ignored by Greek writers. "The Druids tell us that the serpents eject these eggs into the air by their hissing, and that a person must be ready to catch them in a cloak, so as not to let them touch the ground..." You then have to ride off as fast as possible until separated from the pursuing serpents by water. There is more fanciful detail, the gist of which seems to be to portray the Druids as mere conjurers. Pliny says that he himself has seen one of the eggs, though he does not say where.

To be taken more seriously are his remarks about the decline of Druidism, a passage which introduces the political attitude of the Romans to the Druids of Gaul. The Romans saw the survival of superstition and primitive ritual as being anti-Roman and conducive to a dangerous spirit of nationalism. They were keen to convince themselves of the benefits bestowed by Rome in stamping them out.

> The Gallic provinces were also pervaded by magic arts, even as recently as living memory, since it was the Emperor Tiberius who suppressed the Druids, and all the host of wizards and healers. But why should I make further mention of these prohibitions, concerning an art which has now crossed the Ocean itself, and has penetrated to the void recesses [*inane*, 'empty space'] of nature. (N2)

Even today, he says, the people of Britannia, with fascination, foster the druidic art – which he has stated had gone there from Gaul, and survived there presumably because of lesser Roman influence. This is one of only three references – the others being Caesar's, already quoted, and Tacitus shortly to be dealt with – to the existence of druidism in Britain. For Caesar the cult was invented in Britain and brought to Gaul;

42

for Pliny however it was the other way round. Finally Pliny reveals his true bias and his tendency to propaganda:

> ...we cannot too highly appreciate the debt that is due to the Roman people, for havng put an end to those monstrous rites, in accordance with which to murder a man was to do an act of the greatest devoutness and to eat his flesh was to secure the highest blessing of health.

The Druids had been accused of human sacrifice before, as we have seen, but it was attributed to exceptional circumstances. Certainly this ritual was regarded by the Romans with extreme disapproval, in spite of the near-sacrificial events in the Colosseum. Cannibalism appears to be a new accusation. The Druids now seem, in the Roman writings, to have gone all the way from wise teachers to savages. It is assumed that as the empire expanded anything which fostered nationalism in the conquered regions was to be increasingly feared, and there seems no doubt that Druidism was the supreme nationalistic force. This we shall now see is also revealed by Tacitus.

Tacitus tells us in *Agricola*, his book about the Romans in Britain, that Britain and Gaul had "the same ritual, the same religious beliefs", and so we may suppose that what Caesar and other sources available to him said about the Gauls applied (as far as Tacitus knew) to the British also. He does not specifically mention the Druids here, but he certainly does so in the Annals, and there we find the only direct reference to there having been Druids in Britain, and even this reference is confined to the isle of Anglesey, which was at the time subject to strong Irish influence, perhaps might even be described as an Irish colony.

Suetonius Paulinus had been newly appointed governor of Britain when he decided to invade Anglesey. In *Agricola* Tacitus had described this decision as being caused by the fact that that island "was feeding the national resistance". In the Annals he offers a more personal motive for Suetonius, that of competing with his contemporary Corbulo. He adds that Anglesey ('Mona') had given sanctuary to many refugees.

Flat-bottomed boats took the infantry across from the Caernarfon coast, while the cavalry-men swam besides their horses. The population of the island lined the other bank in a dense mass. Black-robed women with dishevelled hair ran among them brandishing torches. The Druids were drawn up in a group and as the Roman fleet landed they raised their hands to heaven and screamed dreadful curses.

So shocked were the legionaries by this unfamiliar sight that they hesitated, imobilised on the beach. With some urging from their general they followed their standard-bearers on, and enveloped the mob with the flames of their own torches. Suetonius cut down "the groves devoted to Mona's barbarous superstitions. For it was their religion to drench their altars with the blood of prisoners and consult their gods by means of human entrails." It is pointed out (by Nora Chadwick) that Tacitus does not say here that the Druids practised human sacrifice, merely that the people of Anglesey at that time did so; but I think the implication is clear that the Druids were involved in these practices. The chief clue to this is that the 'barbarous' rituals were connected with the groves, as, according to several Roman sources, so were the Druids.

There is, however, no physical evidence of the Druids having been there, so we have only this one testimony of Tacitus to support the claim. The remarkable hoard found apparently cast into the water of Llyn Cerrig Bach is often suggested as evidence for religious activity on Anglesey, but as Frances Lynch says in her invaluable book *Prehistoric Anglesey*: "Any connection between the sacred pool of Llyn Cerrig Bach and the Druids is speculative...."; and there are suggestions for the explanation of the find in non-religious terms. (N3)

It was, among all these later Roman writings, the work of Pliny which has been the most influential on our present understanding, and that is ironically because it was published among much else from the considerable collection by Iolo Morganwg, as part of the two volume edition called *Barddas*, which came out after his death, in 1862 and 1874. Here he gives the passages from Pliny referred to above, with some notes regarding the detail of the Druids' use of oak groves, of the mistletoe ("All admit that this plant was in great repute among the Ancient Cymry"), and the white robes: "the official dress of the British Druids".

Edward Williams, now known by his bardic name Iolo Morganwg, was a stonemason born in Glamorgan in 1747 who worked in his home county and in London, where he attended meetings of the Gwyneddigion Society, an early gathering of the London Welsh. He was no ordinary stonemason, being a highly talented poet in both English and Welsh and a studious collector of medieval and later manuscripts. He was also, from an early age, addicted to laudanum, a derivative of opium, which seems in the end to have affected his mental condition. All the evidence is that he became unable to distinguish reality from fantasy. Iolo became so obsessed with the idea of the antiquity of the Welsh people that he began to invent evidence of it, and in doing so became a major influence of the antiquarian revival of the late 18th century.

Modern-day Druids still wear the robes attributed to them by Iolo Morganwg in the eighteenth century

Iolo invented, among other things, something which is now called neo-Druidism, taking some clues from Pliny to dress his re-discovered Druids in white robes, which, ironically, they still wear. He drew up the ritual for the Gorsedd ceremony, holding the first meeting of the 'Order of Bards', *Gorsedd Beirdd Ynys Prydain*, on Primrose Hill in London, in June 1792. The culmination of his disinformation campaign came when the Gorsedd which he had invented was adopted by the incipient national-eisteddfod at an eisteddfod held at the Ivy Bush, Carmarthen, in 1819.

Many of the genuine manuscripts in Iolo's huge collection were 'improved' by him with the aim of supporting his cause. Some were simply his own work. So convincing was he that for about a hundred years scholars accepted the misinformation which Iolo had invented. Doubts were beginning to be expressed in the 1920s, by, for instance, Professor John Morris-Jones at Bangor University, but it was not until 1926, when the Iolo archive became lodged with the National Library of Wales and the literary historian G. J. Williams (whose life's work the disentanglement then became) was appointed to examine it, that the extent of the damage became clear. From about 1926, when Williams's conclusions were published, Iolo is ultimately exposed as a fabricator and forger. By then it was, in many ways, too late. People always prefer fiction to fact, and the fiction, regarding the Druids, was already established by Iolo during his lifetime in the 18th century and had taken firm root in the British imagination, where it still flourishes. The Gorsedd rituals which Iolo invented are still basically those which are enacted every year in connection with the National Eisteddfod, and various orders of Druids meet (for instance at Stonehenge) for solstice sunrises wearing the clothes Iolo designed for them.

Antiquarianism was a strange movement, possibly owing

something to a fear of the future engendered by the beginnings of the Industrial Revolution, a sort of cultural Luddism. Artists such as Rossetti and Burne-Jones, writers such as Tennyson, turned (in the aftermath of Iolo's movement) for some of their subject matter to an idealised British past which owed a great deal to the Celtic revival. It is to such a fairy-story world that the reincarnated Druids belong.

And yet... And yet there are a few things we can claim to know about the Druids, only a few, but these pieces fall into a coherent pattern. The Druids were the repository of traditional knowledge, which they kept to themselves. They left no written records. They believed in the immortality of the soul, and its passage from one being to another at death. They studied the stars. They taught, and people studied to join their number. They acted as arbitrators and peacemakers in disputes. The religion which they taught either began or ended up in Britain. The Romans set out to curb their cult, and the last we hear of them is a mass slaughter under Roman invasion in Anglesey, in AD 61.

It was said that Anglesey at that time was a haven for refugees. It is probable that if there were Druids in other parts of Britain these would have been amongst those who fled there during this period of Roman entrenchment and in the knowledge of the determination to stamp out their teachings. Thus perhaps some thousands of years of wisdom were obliterated in one summer afternoon, on the Menai shore.

It is not in fact known how long the Druids had been a part of Celtic civilisation, so we do no know whether they had been passing on traditional knowledge for long enough to convey the secrets (as they are to us) of the standing stones, the cromlechs, and the stone circles. What we do know about is the frustration of being confronted with things so apparently obvious yet so opaque. Somebody must have known, we feel, yet the hiatus in the conveyance of this knowledge yawns between us. How could it have been so completely forgotten, when we still remember, in our lore, the great floods at the end of the last Ice Age, and the trauma of the discovery of agriculture? Could the answer be that it was systematically wiped out, with sword and fire, somewhere near Brynsiencyn?

Anglesey shore from Caernarfon quay

If so, perhaps some people escaped. Perhaps some of them there were in the long process of learning the Druidic wisdom. Perhaps they had an imperfect understanding of it. There were one or two of the great Iron Age hillforts which the Romans had left standing, as being, presumably, irrelevant to the conquered areas and too much of a problem to be worth their attention. One of these is Tre'r Geiri, at the neck of the Llyn peninsula, within site of this Anglesey shore.

There are two things which are unusual about Tre'r Geiri, apart from the fact that it is the only hillfort in this area which the Romans left intact. One is that its compound contains about a hundred and fifty huts, whereas most hillforts have few, and some none. So it was inhabited, indeed densely populated. The other fact about it which requires explanation is that it dates from the first century AD until the fourth, that

Tre'r Ceiri, aerial view

Tre'r Ceiri, detail of huts

is, precisely related to the Roman advance and presence. Most hillforts are earlier, and had begun to fall out of use by then. When the Romans finally withdrew from Segontium, at Caernarfon nearby, Tre'r Geiri was of no further use, and it was then depopulated. The fullest extent of its use was the century after Suetonius's invasion.

If there were refugees from Anglesey and from Britain in general who escaped from the Roman suppression, and if any druidic wisdom escaped from the Anglesey slaughter, it must inevitably have been to the crowded safety of Tre'r Geiri that they came. It is there (for lack of an alternative) that the spirit of native Welshness survived, unblemished by the imposition of an alien order.

After the coming of Christianity there was no room for belief in the gods of the old religion, and (as happened in Greece, in Scandinavia, in the Americas, indeed elsewhere) the themes of the old religion became stories. It must be said that a little of what the Druids were said to have taught may in fact reappear in the stories of the Mabinogion. The doctrine of the indestructible, transmigrating soul, for instance, is recognisable in the transformation of Lleu, on death, into an eagle, and Bodeuwedd into an owl; perhaps it also lingers in the saga of the conflict of Ceridwen and Gwion Bach, in which they each become a succession of different creatures until the final crucial rebirth. Perhaps also the druidic role of arbitrating peace is distantly reflected in the part played by Gwydion and Math, the 'wizards', in negotiating a cease-fire between the armies of north and south Wales when these met, in the tale of *Mab fab Mathonwy*, on Traeth Mawr. Perhaps after all something did survive.

Bibliography

Nora K. Chadwick, *The Druids*. University of Wales Press, 1966.

Strabo, *Geography*. iv. 4.

Diodorus Siculus. 31. 2,

Julius Caesar, *The Conquest of Gaul*. I. 1. Trs. S. A. Handforth, Penguin 1951.

Ronald Hutton. *The Pagan Religions of the Ancient British Isles*. BCA , 1991.

Pliny. *Natural History*. Book xvi.

Tacitus. *Agricola*. 11.

Tacitus. *Annals*. xiv. 27-30. Trs. Michael Grant. *The Annals of Imperial Rome*. Penguin, 1956.

Frances Lynch. *Prehistoric Anglesey*. The Anglesey Antiquarian Society, 1991.

The Barddas of Iolo Morganwg, Vol. 1., ed. J. Williams ab Ithel.

N1. The Greek word for 'oak' is *drus* and the term 'druid' also seems connected with words for 'oak' in Welsh (*derw*) and early Irish (*drui*) and this may indicate an ancient connection in the depths of the Indo-European mother-language, but the matter remains obscure. See Chadwick, *op.cit*. pp. 12-13.

N2. There is some possibility that Pliny was confusing his emperors. It was Augustus, Tiberius' predecessor and father-in-law, who prohibited druidical practices for Roman citizens, which included the people in Gaul who had adopted citizenship – but not the Druids themselves, who seem to have suffered no direct suppression. Chadwick *op.cit*. p.72.

N3. For instance T. P. Roberts, The International Journal of Nautical Archeology (2002) pp.25-38.

3

The Anglo-Saxon Invasion

The Venerable Bede set the form of much of our received history, the version we are taught in school, and he it was, in his great work *Historiam Ecclesiasticam Gentis Anglorum*, 'A History of the English Church and People', written in Jarrow in AD 731, who gave us as the first event of our story

Bede (from a Nuremberg chronicle)

as a nation the idea of the *adventus Saxonum*, the Saxon arrival. Actually Bede took much of his information from Gildas, who wrote in the sixth century, within a generation of the ending of the period to which he refers. Sometimes Bede is hardly even paraphrasing Gildas, merely copying him out.

According to Bede, from Gildas, the process of invasion went as follows. The country had for a long time been suffering from attacks by the Picts (from the north) and the

Scots (from Ireland). In the devastated aftermath of a severe plague the attacks of the northern invaders were renewed with fresh determination. A council was held, and a crucial error made. 'All agreed with their king, Vortigern, to call for the help of the Saxon people over the sea'.

They came in three long ships, *tribus longis navibus*. The king gave them lands in the eastern part of the island, and they fulfilled their side of the bargain by defeating the northern hosts. At the same time they sent word back home: of the fertility of the island, and the slothfulness (*segnitia*) of the Britons.

A large fleet came, with an army of warriors. They intimidated the natives and before long, now allied with the Picts, increased their demands for land and provisions as a pretext for rebellion. This then followed at once. The 'impious conquerors depopulated the nearby cities and farmlands, from the eastern to the western sea, without resistance, spreading their fire, until nearly the whole of the lost island was covered over '.

This story was filled out by Nennius, who wrote a History of Britain (combining indiscriminantly folk legend and chronicled record), about 800 AD; and an even fuller and more imaginitive version was developed, from this, by Geoffrey of Monmouth in *The History of the Kings of Britain*, in the first half of the twelth century. In Nennius the people involved are named and identified, the king of the Britons, Vortigern, on the one hand, and the brothers Hengist and Horsa on the other. It must be said that 'Vortigern' is now considered to be a title rather than a name, meaning High King, and that Hengist and Horsa are not considered to be historical figures.

Nennius has the wily Saxons winning from Vortigern more lands, and importing more and more of their people. It is Geoffrey of Monmouth who supplies the full melodrama of the 'night of the long knives', the slaughter of the unarmed

Britons and the flight of Vortigern. These elements of pantomime are of interest to us, seeking historical fact, as examples of the way in which the tales become increasingly personalised in the course of their long transmission, in this case from Gildas to Bede to Nennius to Geoffrey.

Although it was reasonable for Bede to think Gildas was reliable, much scholarship on the subject has subsequently released doubts. These come in two forms: as to the single authorship of the work itself (*De Excidio Britonum*) and hence its date; and as to the intentions of the author. Briefly, it has been argued first that the 'history' section of the work, as opposed to its epistolary, polemic content, is a much later interpolation, and hence less valuable as a primary source. A second, quite different attack has it that the author was not at any point trying to write history, but to assemble arguments for a religious manifesto. All this is good literary fun, but it need not concern us much here, since the coming of the Saxons can be shown, from other hard evidence, to have been quite unlike the version conveyed by Gildas/Bede into our history.

There is much significant evidence that by the late phases of Roman presence in Britain Germanic groups had been settled here for some time, and that their arrival had been more a matter of gradual and peaceful assimilation than of invasion. Also, that it had its roots not in the hiatus left by the final Roman withdrawal but in the organised and highly controlled conditions of the height of the Roman occupation.

From the very start of the conquest of Britain, indeed in the original invading force itself in AD 43, there were Germanic cohorts within the Roman army. They were still present three to four hundred years later, in the garrison defending Hadrian's Wall, in the third and fourth centuries,

Hadrian's Wall at Greenhead's Lough

now among many other European nationalities. They were known as Bavarians in the early days, the later divisions such as Angles, Saxons and Jutes perhaps not yet recognised. This began to change in the third century, when some of the recruited cohorts come to be known as Frisians. These Germanic tribes were there for several generations, with the implication that they would inevitably have mated with native women. Already by then the genetic separation of German and Celt must, in some areas, have been becoming unclear.

Germans, by then known as *Alemanni*, were present in large numbers at York in 306, when they were instrumental in bringing about the succession of Constantine the Great.

Already by 372, according to the later Roman historian Ammianus Marcellinus, German groups were being displaced from continental Europe and seeking haven in Britain not just for militaristic reasons but because of over-crowding and the tendency for the resulting competition to lead to war, factors which generally lie somewhere near the root of the causes of migration.

Such slight and tentative archaeological evidence as has come to light suggests settlements in the east Yorkshire area. Early Saxon cemeteries are also found in connection with the Roman road system in northern Norfolk and Lincolnshire.

Archaeological evidence in the form of their funerary rites indicates that the earliest settlers kept in touch with their homelands, and if unsettled circumstances still prevailed there it is likely that they would start to arrive in increasing numbers; and certainly we know that sometime during the fourth century, in the last phase of Roman Britain, their incursions became a problem. We know this because they gave rise to the foundation of a chain of Roman forts, stretching from the Solent to the Wash, on what was then officially termed the *Litus Saxonicum*, the Saxon Shore. Our

The Saxon shore

Roman forts on the Channel coast and the North Sea

knowledge of the name dates from a document of around 408 AD, but the scheme appears to belong to the first part of the fourth century. Nine forts are named and have been identified (for instance at Dover, Lympne, Pevensey and Porchester) built in a distinctive form which makes them a definable set, and their purpose is clear. Unlike the earlier Channel forts they are not suited to be supply bases for the Roman fleet, but now, with their orientation towards the North Sea as well as the Channel coasts, show a different emphasis, that of coastal protection.

If this was its intention the scheme failed. Its failure becomes apparent almost at once, with the incidence of signs of permanent Saxon settlements along the eastern coastline during the fourth century. The term 'Saxon Shore' in fact perhaps began then to change its meaning. Officially recognised, it seems, at first as an area of defence to keep them out, it became accepted as the land they had effectively colonised.

They started settling along the coastal strip, which indicates that they came as raiding parties first – though it must be said that some authorities claim to see in the pattern of settlement signs of an organised army. It was not long before they spread inland. It is interesting to find from the archaeology that these people appeared to have Saxon cultural origins (as the name given to their coastline by the Romans implies) in the very areas, such as East Anglia and even north to the Humber, which were later undoubtedly occupied by Angles. Right from the start the matter is more complex than we might have thought.

It is perhaps a fallacy, or an exaggeration, to think of a native population being dislodged or displaced from their lands by these, or indeed by later, settlers. A glance at the comparative archaeological maps shows that the parts they settled were almost empty. This might be for technical archaeological reasons – the settlements of the natives left no traces? – but it would still be in sharp contrast to the rest of the country, south and west.

Unless the archaeological record is greatly distorted, then, there were a few minor lake settlements in North Yorkshire in the Iron Age, almost nothing further north; the Fenland was uninhabited, and across the whole of the Midlands there were less than a dozen small enclosed ring forts. The settlement on the Wrekin was about the furthest east we find anything by way of major structure at this time.

To the west of the Severn things were completely different. There are more significant sites between the Clwyd valley and the Shropshire plain than there are in the whole area between the Wrekin and the Wash. In the south-west things were different too, and although to the east Kent was sparsely populated the bulk of the Iron Age population of Britain seems to have lived between the Solent and the Severn estuary.

To some extent the Romans changed all that. The level

lands of the eastern Midlands better suited their military strategies and their infrastructure than the mountainous west. They built roads across the Fens and founded cities in the eastern valleys. They and the warming climate started the process of draining the fens: the Romans appear to have dug a long dyke for drainage, and during at least a period of their time there it is now thought (from tree-ring analysis) that there was a period of much warmer weather. It was into this world recently deserted by the Romans that the first settlers arrived, far from the largely unromanised British in their western heartland. Such Celtic remains as are found in the territories occupied by the newcomers indicates a process of assimilation and integration. Excavations carried out in 1974 and 5 by Oxford Archaeology, for instance, investigating a gravel pit in Oxfordshire, revealed an Anglo-Saxon cemetery dating from the mid fifth century to the early seventh, where out of a total of some seventy burials found there it was established (from analysis of tooth enamel) that only five percent of those buried originated from outside the local area. We thus have evidence of a mixed immigrant-native community, suggesting harmonious co-existence rather than slaughter or flight as the typical ground of this invasion.

Of course there is evidence of pre-Roman occupation of parts of the east, such as by the Iceni, a notable Romanised tribe based in what is now Norfolk, who had been there for perhaps a hundred years by the time they rebelled against the Romans under their queen Boudica, in AD 61. What is noted here is that the characteristic major settlements do not cluster, on the east coast, as they do elsewhere – and that there is no need to hypothesise that the Celts were forced into the mountainous west, since there is anyway ample evidence that they had been there, by then, for thousands of years.

The 1982 book *The Anglo-Saxons* was edited and part-written by James Campbell, and in it Campbell regrets the lack of clarity in the evidence for how much of Britain was in Anglo-Saxon hands by the middle sixth century. The Britons, he says, are elusive archaeologically. Perhaps it is "because they did not bury grave goods, so that their graves are unrecognizable"? He also speculates that "it may hardly have been possible by the sixth century to tell a man of German descent from one of British". After so much time during which they are assumed to have intermarried this would not be surprising. There is even confusion in the recorded dynasties: the Saxon kings of Wessex had an apparently British ancestor, Cerdic, and this anomaly seems to have pre-existed their coming to Britain; Saxon or Anglian kingdoms may in some or perhaps most cases have been take-overs of earlier British ones, rather than new foundations; and "It may be some or many Anglo-Saxon kings had British wives."

There remains the matter of the language – but that does not seem to have presented the barrier we might expect. The Anglo-Saxon kings of the new kingdoms of Bernicia and Deira were probably bilingual. The sons of Aethelfrith, king of Bernicia, brought up amongst the Picts and the Scots, spoke both northern languages. Likewise Edwin, king of Deira, was brought up in exile in Anglesey, and so inevitably spoke British. When these kingdoms merged to form Northumbria Bede tells us with evident approval that King Oswald ruled over people who spoke between them "the four languages", implying I think that Oswald spoke all four himself: British, Pictish, Scottish and English. (N1) In any case sharing a language proved to be no guarantee of harmony. During much of the time we are considering the greatest conflict was not between the Celtic-speaking and the

Germanic-speaking peoples, but between the Angles of Mercia and the Angles of Northumbria.

Whatever was the mechanism by which they came into existence – whether consolidation of raiding-party settlements or conquest of existing systems – Anglo-Saxon kingdoms in Britain developed fast, during the late sixth century.

During this period we hear of some encounters with the British, and then more often of alliances with them. The Anglo-Saxon chroniclers (dependent for their early records on Bede, writing, themselves, a century or so after him) give some slight details of early warfare which Bede does not mention. Thus very early on, in the year 491, we hear of a slaughter of the British near Pevensey, on the Sussex coast. A further encounter is reported in 495, when a party landed at a place called Cerdicesora, which it is speculated was on Southampton Water. And in 501 a battle took place between another invading force and the natives at Portsmouth. In the course of following the foundation of Wessex we hear of battles against the British in the area of the Isle of Wight. By 552 the conflict has spread to Salisbury, and by 556 to Barbury. We hear about the foundation of Northumbria meanwhile, but nothing about the Northumbrian Angles fighting the British. All the conflict during the mid-sixth century is in the south. By the 570s it had reached as far as Aylesbury. In 577 by a victory at the notable battle of Dyrham, near Bristol, in which three British kings were killed and the cities of Bath, Cirencester and Gloucester fell to Wessex, the fast-expanding new kingdom had (as John Davies points out) reached the shores of the Severn estuary.

In the rest of the country it is clear that the invading settlers spent at least some of their time fighting each other.

In 568 the king of Wessex fought the Kentish king at Wimbledon, forcing him to retreat into Kent. And we are told of Ceowulf, who began to reign in Wessex in 597, that he always "fought and strove with the Angles, the Picts or the Scots" .

A crucial defeat of a British force took place in northern Yorkshire in about 600 – crucial because it decimated the strongest of the tribes in northern Britain and so began the confinement of resistance in Wales. It is not stated explicitly that the reason the Gododdin tribe went to war was the recognition of the threat of the merger of Deira and Bernicia, but it is clear that some such immediate crisis impelled them. Catraeth, against which place they marched, is the modern Catterick, and so can be seen to lie in a central position with regard to the emerging Northumbria. The battle of Catraeth is preserved for us by the great epic poem *Y Gododdin*, attributed to the early British poet Aneirin, in which the brave and famous, but doomed, heroes are celebrated. It is, to say the least, unusual for such a grandly heroic poem to commemorate a devastating defeat, but the theme of the poem is that only three men came back from the battle, the poet among them: *a minnau o'm gwaetffrau gwerth fy ngwenwawd.* 'And I from my bleeding for the sake of my song.'

Some strange and seemingly random alliances came about in the course of the fragmented development of kingdoms. The unification of Deira and Bernicia by Aethelfrith in 604 had the effect of conjoining the interests of Gwynedd and Deira, since the heir to the Deira throne, Edwin, then still a child, was taken for his safety to the court of King Cadfan of Gwynedd, in Anglesey. When he grew up he wanted his kingdom back, moved into Cheshire to seek

Mercian help, and so launched a rivalry between two power-blocks of Angles. It was thus that the complicated grouping of alliances at the Battle of Chester in 616 or 617 arose, when Aethelfrith moved his army south to block the extension of the Gwynedd-Mercian alliance.

The Battle of Chester was not fought between the Anglo-Saxons and the Welsh, as is generally supposed. The main part of the Welsh army under Cadfan of Gwynedd was not even there. They arrived after the battle was over, in time to pursue the retreating Northumbrians. The Welsh had been represented at the battle by Selyf king of Powys, who, being nearer to the location, got there in time to bear the worst of the assault. Their losses accounted for the long weakness of their kingdom which followed. Aethelfrith fled homewards with his Northumbrians but the lands he had to pass through were consistently hostile, and the king was ambushed by the East Angles near Bawtry in Yorkshire. Having killed Aethelfrith they put Edwin on the throne of Northumbria. It is ironic that the Battle of Chester is usually represented as a victory of the English over the Welsh.

This was not to be the end of the dispute between Mercia and Northumbria, which continued with Gwynedd on the Mercian side. Once in power, Edwin turned on his old allies, including Cadwallon (now king of Gwynedd, having succeeded his father Cadfan in 625). An invasion by Edwin (once his foster-brother) forced Cadwallon to take refuge in Ireland.

The confusion continued. Cadwallon, returning from exile in 633, joined forces with the Anglian king of Mercia, Penda, in an anti-Edwin league. This powerful grouping went north-east to confront their opponent, which they did so forcibly that they defeated and killed him, at Doncaster, in October

633. The two amalgamated forces then ravaged Northumbria for a year. But it was not over yet.

After Edwin's death there was an apparent gap in the ruling of Northumbria, and sure enough a leader emerged to fill it. Oswald was a younger son of Aethelfrith, Edwin's enemy, and during Edwin's rule he and his brothers had been in exile in Scotland. When they re-emerged in Northumbria the older brothers were killed by Cadwallon, so that Oswald was the inheritor of the throne of Bernicia. He confronted Cadwallon at a place afterwards called Heavenfield, near Hexham in the Tyne valley. There he personally killed Cadwallon.

This succession of related battles continues, since once again the Mercians allied with the men of Gwynedd and Powys. When Penda went home and joined forces with the Welsh Oswald knew this to be a dangerous alliance. He took an army south to try to break the coalition. But perhaps he was too far from home, his lines overstretched. At a place called Maserfeld he was defeated and killed, on 5th August 642 (Bede tells us), aged thirty-eight. We know that Maserfeld was at or near Oswestry (a natural location for an attempt to split Gwynedd, Powys and Mercia) since that town takes its name from the cross set up there to commemorate Oswald's death, known later as 'Oswald's Tree'. (N2)

Penda survived, and after a brief exile he re-appeared in Northumbria, once again assisted by the Welsh. They got as far as the ancient capital at Bamburgh, at which point the new king, Oswiu, tried to bribe them to go home. A battle took place which Oswiu won, and when Penda found himself deserted by the Welsh he fled to Yorkshire, and was caught and killed by Oswiu at Leeds. This was crucial, since Oswiu now ruled Mercia as well as Northumbria, a position which he reinforced by marrying his daughter to Penda's son. The Angles could now do without the help of the Welsh, since the combined kingdom was vast and prosperous, and in fact it was at this point that parts of Shropshire were acquired from Powys.

Such a union could not be maintained at that time, and Mercia in due course revived and asserted independence. For a time it seemed as if the two kingdoms, Gwynedd and Mercia, were to find a common destiny in holding off the encroachment of Wessex, but this too broke down when Mercia became a dominant force in the eighth century under its ambitious king Offa. At Langport in Somerset, meanwhile, under the leadership of Gereint son of Erbin, Prince of Devon, what appears to be a successful British assault took place in 710, in which however Gereint died. The surviving Welsh poem *Gereint Filius Erbin* is a lament for him, in which there is an early mention of Arthur, who appears to have been in direct command of the troops – *ameraudur* (cognate with 'imperator', in the sense of 'commander-in-chief') *llywiaudir llawer* ('a director of toil'). This passage is however thought by some to be an interpolation from a later text.

Langport is called Llongborth in the Welsh verse, meaning 'ship haven', and is a term which was used to describe harbours used by the Vikings. A new problem, that of the Viking raids from Scandinavia and Dublin, with further changeable alliances between Welsh, Danes, and Mercians, began to concern the kings both of England and Wales, and Rhodri Mawr, one of the few princes who have ruled almost all of Wales, had his power stretched in several directions. He became king of Gwynedd in 844, and he died in a battle against the Mercians in 878. That and its successor

66

are the most explicit encounters between the Welsh and the English of this combative period, and the last of this phase. Ten years after Rhodri's death his son Anarawd defeated a Mercian army on the banks of the Conwy river, rare evidence of Mercia's westerly incursions. The late battle was one of the few of which it might be said that the Welsh fought the English. It was known as *Dial Rhodri*, Rhodri's Revenge, since the Welsh won.

Bibiography

Bede. *A History of the English Church and People*. Leo Sherley-Price (tr.) Penguin, 1968.

N. J. Higham. *The Northern Counties to AD 1000*. Longman. 1986.

N. J. Higham. *The English Conquest*. Manchester University Press. 1994.

John Morris (ed. & tr.) *Nennius, British History and The Welsh Annals*. Phillimore, 1980.

Dr Andrew Millard *et al.* 'Anglo-Saxon Cemetery Results Question Violent Invasion Theory.' Journal of Archaeological Science, Oxford Archaeology. February 26th, 2014.

James Campbell (ed.) *The Anglo-Saxons*. Book Club Associates. 1982.

Anne Savage (ed. & tr.) *The Anglo-Saxon Chronicles*. Book Club Associates.

Gwyn Williams (ed.) *The Burning Tree*. Faber. 1961.

(N1) *Denique omnes nationes et prouincias Brittaniae, quae in IIII linguas, id est Brettonum, Pictorum, Scottorum, et Anglorum, diuisae sunt, in dicione accepit.*

(N2). The material in these paragraphs is dealt with more fully in my book *North Wales in the Making*. Gwasg Carreg Gwalch. 1995. pp. 101- 9.

4

The Arthurian Themes

It is a mistake to think that if there are two apparently contradictory ways of describing something, one must be right and the other wrong. There is often more than one equally valid way of looking at things, as for instance a geologist and a landscape artist will look at a valley, say, in different ways, yet each, within their terms of reference, are equally right. So if we recognise that in the cases of characters such as Arthur and Merlin there are two quite distinct strands of identity, the factual and the romantic, this is not to say that one is more real, more authentic, than the other.

Because part of the point of this book is to identify what the facts of the matter are, I intend to deal first with the facts, and then to investigate how they became transformed into the elaborate archetypes in which form they are better known. First, **Arthur**.

What distinguishes Arthur from figures of mainstream history, say Julius Caesar or Alexander the Great, is the almost evasive way the early records treat him. The references seem to suggest that we already know the facts about him, and public records such as the Anglo-Saxon Chronicle do not mention him at all. As it happens there are clear indications that Arthur was not just a fictional character, and there is a credible reason for his having been omitted from official national history. Disappointingly perhaps for those who love a mystery, not much about Arthur turns out to be mysterious.

The earliest documents which refer to him are mostly hard to date precisely, since we only have them in the form of medieval manuscripts, whereas they clearly belong in origin to a much earlier period. There is (we shall see) the 'History' of Nennius, written about the year 800 but from older sources (so the author says), and available to us in several manuscripts, the oldest and best of which dates from about 1100. The Nennius account of Arthur is brief but clear, and it provides the source for the assumption that Arthur fought the Saxons. First, in the same year as the death of Hengest, King of the people of Kent, *De Arturo rege belligero et de duodecim bellis, quae adversus Saxones habuit...* 'Concerning the warlike king Arthur, and the twelve battles, which he had against the Saxons, and of the image of St Mary, in which he triumphed, and of how many of his enemies he laid low in one assault.' The reference to the holy Mary is obscure, but the evidence is that already by the time the author compiled his history there were stories about King Arthur's remarkable achievements circulating in popular lore. This is from the summary calendar, and a fuller description in the same document adds that it was nine hundred and sixty men who fell in one day, "and no one laid them low save he alone, and he was victorious in all his battles". Earlier in that same entry the author had used words which must be regarded as the gist of the record of the subject by Nennius: "*Tunc Arthur pugnabat contra illos in illis diebus cum regibus Brittonum, sed ipse dux erat bellorum.*" 'Then Arthur fought against them in those days with the kings of the Britons. But he was the leader of the battles.' Much has been made of the titles mentioned here, but it does not follow from the mention of the kings either that he himself was, or was not, a king. The designation 'dux' might be an official one, as if 'dux bellorum' was a national post, like 'commander in chief' of the British forces, equivalent to the position held in Roman time by the 'Comes Britanniarum', the Count of Britain, who led the mobile forces. That accords well with the view of Arthur as a cavalry commander, which is suggested by the wide spread of the traditional locations of his battles. There is, however, no need to see the word 'dux' as a title. The document is not Roman, and that it is written in Latin does not necessarily mean that the writer would have been familiar with Roman military titles. 'Dux' means simply 'leader', and all that we can read from this is that Arthur, rather than any of the others, led the battles. He might have been a king or simply a soldier, as he is referred to elsewhere in the same literature.

Nennius makes no other mention of Arthur's exploits as historical campaigner, and the only other mention in his work is in a list of 'Wonders' of Britain added to his chronicle. Here it is said that a footprint of his dog Cabal – *canis Arthuri militis*, the dog of Arthur the soldier – may be seen in the area of Builth, indicating for us that the purely folkloric aspect of the hero had already begun to take over. The epithet 'the soldier' however also occurs later in the same 'Wonder', when a tomb is said to be that of Amr, 'a son of Arthur the soldier'.

The Welsh Annals, known as *Annales Cambriae*, because of course they were written in Latin, are extant in the same manuscript as Nennius (known as British Library MS Harleian 3859), and in others, but their content is agreed to be of greater antiquity. They are monastic work, church annals put together for religious-calendar purposes, and it is likely that the entries were made originally in the year to which they referred. Thus (although the earliest manuscript which we have of the Annals dates to the same time as the 'History' of Nennius, that is, about 1100, and so of course had been copied many times and no doubt added to and altered in the process) it is possible that they represent our oldest source for Arthur.

And so it is of utmost interest for us to read there that in the year 516 was fought the Battle of Badon, "in which Arthur carried the Cross of our Lord Jesus Christ for three days and three nights on his shoulders, and the Britons were the victors." The reference is to a shield or livery, no doubt, but it tells us of a Christian victory against those we might suppose to be heathens. A little later, 537, we hear of "The Battle of Camlann, in which Arthur and Medraut fell; and there was plague in Britain and Ireland." It is not said who Medraut was, or whether he died at Camlann supporting or opposing Arthur; but the later tradition that Arthur fell in battle against his nephew Mordred points irresistably to the supposition that here is the earliest seed of the tragic end.

If Arthur and Medraut were opponents, and both apparently British rather than invaders, then we have commemorated in the Annals at this point the long-standing theme that the inhabitants of Britain, once left to themselves, fought each other. Indeed our earliest historical source, Gildas, writing in the second half of the sixth century, says explicitly that "External wars may have stopped, but not civil ones", in his own day.

Since the rough date at which he wrote is secure from internal evidence, it is clear that Gildas would have been a contemporary of Arthur, if Arthur were really a military figure of the sixth century. Since he dealt in detail with the exploits of his time Gildas naturally dealt with the Battle of Badon, in fact in some detail. 'From then on victory went now to our countrymen, now to their enemies... This lasted right up till the siege of Badon Hill, pretty well the last defeat of the villains, and certainly not the least. That was the year of my birth; as I know, one month of the forty-fourth year since then has already passed.' Yet although the Welsh Annals firmly ascribe the victory of Badon to Arthur, Gildas, whom we might have thought was as good a source, says that the leader in that battle was Ambrosius, a Romanised British leader – 'who, perhaps alone of the Romans, had survived the shock of this notable storm...' The fact that he has quite a lot to say about Ambrosius makes us confront the major anomaly of his book, and its implications. He does not mention Arthur at all.

This omission is important because it can be taken to indicate that Arthur did not exist. Gildas was writing the history of his own time, and it does not seem from his work that Arthur occurred within that. This is the root of Arthur's ambiguous position: he is not quite of the same type as historical figures evidenced from contemporary sources. Moreover when Bede wrote his 'History of the English Church and People', in Jarrow in 731, he was working very largely from Gildas. As a result Bede does not mention Arthur either, and our traditional national history is based originally on Bede.

Of course one explanation for this omission could be that Arthur was a later invention, and got added to the other source documents by copying scribes. It must be said, however, that various arguments have been put forward, some more credible than others, explaining why although knowing of Arthur, Gildas chose not to mention him.

It is said, for instance, by current commentators, that

praise of a successful hero would not have served his purpose, which was to use examples of past failures to illustrate the fall from grace of his people. Gildas was writing a polemic, it is said, rather than a history, and we should take his text to be in the manner of a sermon, a warning to the future based on illustrations of disasters from the past. But this line of argument is contradicted by his treatment of Ambrosius, for whom he has nothing but praise.

Maen Huail

The more convincing reasoning is itself rooted in the folklore. It says that Gildas and Arthur knew each other perfectly well, but that they had quarrelled. In the square of the town of Ruthin is a large lump of limestone. It is called Maen Huail, 'Huail's Stone', and the story connected with it appears to be ancient, though our earliest record of it is perhaps that collected by Elis Gruffydd, a soldier, chronicler and translator, in 1530. Huail was one of the sons of Caw, of a Pictish family who came south, perhaps with the tribes led by Cunedda in about 400. He was the elder brother of the historian Gildas.

Arthur and Huail were rivals for the affections of a lady, as a result of which they fought a duel, and Arthur was wounded in the thigh. A reconciliation was agreed, but on one condition demanded by Arthur. There should be no mention in the future about the wound, from which Arthur continued to limp. Years later, in Ruthin, Arthur attended a dance in disguise. Huail, also present, was heard to remark that the dancing was good, apart from the limp. Arthur took this to be a breach of their agreement, and he had Huail beheaded on a convenient stone, "which" (says Lady Charlotte Guest, in her notes to the Mabinogion) "lay in the street of the town.... This stone is still to be seen in the town of Rhuthyn." It has its own niche now in St Peter's Square.

This credible explanation, now much favoured, is not new. Giraldus Cambrensis added to his 'Itinerary Through Wales' a 'Description of Wales', in 1194, in which he mentions Arthur and the Gildas puzzle:

With regard to Gildas, who inveighs so bitterly against his own nation, the Britons affirm that, highly irritated at the death of his brother, the prince of Albania, whom king Arthur had slain, he wrote these invectives, and upon the same occasion threw into the sea many excellent books, in which he had described the actions of Arthur, and the celebrated deeds of his countrymen; from which cause it arises, that no authentic account of so great a prince is any where to be found.

The matter is thus left tantalisingly undecided, since perhaps it is unjust to assume that a personal motive would have been sufficient to impel an apparently serious writer to wipe someone important out of history. There are, as it happens, independent circumstantial indications for supposing Arthur to have been a real figure, or at least for positing his equivalent of that time.

During the twenty or so years after the Battle of Badon there was a noticeable pause in the Saxon advances in Britain. They did not attempt to expand their established territories. Britain was the only place in Europe where this happened: elsewhere they continued to occupy new lands without pause. "I would argue," writes Peter Berresford Ellis, in his 1993 book *Celt and Saxon*, "that many of their most powerful chieftains had been slaughtered at Badon and so they had to rebuild their structures and societies." Geoffrey Ashe had also pointed out, in *From Caesar to Arthur*, in 1960, that Procopius, writing at the court of the Emperor Justinian in Constantinople, about the middle of the sixth century, said that every year "great numbers" of the Saxons of Britain emigrate to Gaul, which they would hardly need to do if their people in Britain had been expanding their settlements.

The earliest Welsh literature supplies some brief but telling references which support the idea of a figure of national reputation. Possibly the earliest, and most tantalising, occurs in *Y Gododdin*, the great epic poem commemorating the northern tribe's defeat at Catraeth, which has been mentioned above. Here it is said of a warrior that 'he was no Arthur', *Cyn ni bai ef Arthur*, meaning presumably that he did not rise to that status. Of course, as always, the phrase might be a late addition, but if it belongs to the original poem by the early Welsh poet Aneirin then it dates from the ninth century. A similar passing reference, which might also be an interpolation, crops up in the poem entitled Gereint Son of Erbin, which was mentioned in the last chapter – Arthur is described as *ameraudur llywiaudir llawur*: the use of the word *ameraudur*, we saw, is not to be seen as a suggestion that Arthur was an emperor, since the Latin word 'imperator', from which it comes, originally means leader, commander-in-chief, just like 'dux'. Even if these literary references were not part of the original text, they are testimony to the fact that by the time their extant manuscripts were produced, in the 13th century, a sufficiently established tradition about Arthur existed for that to be copied into important documents.

In due course this purely military personality begins to acquire a regal status. A number of Saints' Lives emerged from the Abbey of Llancarfan. We have them now in 12th century manuscripts, but some of their material is clearly older. Five Lives mention Arthur, seen from an unfavourable point of view, clearly a potential enemy of the Church. Two

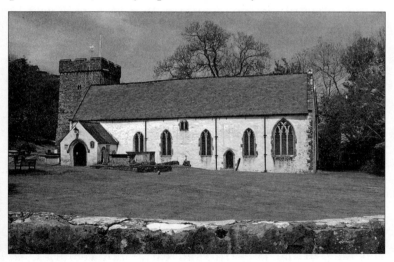

The abbey of Llancarfan produced several 'Lives of Saints' which mention King Arthur

are of special interest for their choice of phrasing. The Life of St Padarn refers to Arthur as 'a certain tyrant', *quidam tyrannus*, although the use of the term 'tyrannus' has to be understood in context. It means 'petty king', perhaps 'upstart ruler', and was the normal way of referring to the many local rulers who sprang up in the absence of central government which succeeded the Roman departure. It is the term used by Gildas, for instance, to summarise the leaders he is attacking.

Caradoc of Llancarfan, with whom the Abbey is mainly connected, himself wrote the Life of Gildas. It is thought to have been written between 1130 and 1150. It contains multiple references to Arthur. Geoffrey Ashe points out that Caradoc's position in the Welsh monastic tradition impels us to take his testimony seriously. Caradoc tells the story of the quarrel between Arthur and Gildas's brother Hueil as a matter of territorial dominance, rather than romance. In contradiction of the folklore version he has Arthur and Gildas as being reconciled. Indeed he makes a point of stressing the friendship between the two: "St Gildas was a contemporary of Arthur, the king of the whole of Britain, whom he loved exceedingly..." In the process of telling the tale he has Arthur visiting Glastonbury, and re-encountering Gildas there – the first connection, Ashe points out, between the hero and his eventual burial place. From our point of view it is of interest that throughout Caradoc refers to Arthur as *rex rebellus*, an insurgent king. 'Rebellus' should perhaps be understood as referring to someone who rekindles a conflict (re-bellus) rather than initiates it.

This awakening of interest in Arthur may be dated generally to the late 11th and early 12th centuries, so coinciding with the great outpouring of Arthur-mania which erupted then, and of interest as forming its context. Up to this point all we have by way of evidence for a factual Arthur is a scattering of suggestions of a military leader of some prowess and reputation. He does not appear to have been associated with a specific territory, let alone to have ruled as an overlord of any particular group. How then, we may wonder, did this figure come to be known as a King, and eventually an Emperor? How does he come by the implied claim to have been our earliest overall leader?

The answer is Geoffrey of Monmouth. Geoffrey completed his great work *The History of the Kings of Britain*, written in Latin, in about 1136, so that Caradoc of Llancarfan was a contemporary of his – and is indeed explicitly referred to by him as such, in one of the extant manuscripts: the king-lists of the subsequent Welsh kings, after the loss of much of Britain to the Saxons, "I leave to my contemporary Caradoc of Llancarfan". Geoffrey's sources are in fact very much the same as ours; he also mentions Gildas and Bede, and the oral tradition. He claims to be translating an ancient book in the British language, and it has been suggested that it was a version of what is now known as Harleian MS 3859, either that text itself or, as

Brit. Mus. Harl. MS. 3859, fol. 188b, ll. 1–25.

The document known as 'Harleian 3859' contains the sources for much early Welsh literature

Lewis Thorpe says in his invaluable Introduction to Geoffrey's work, "something closely related to" it. This manuscript, as we have become aware, is our principal source for Nennius and the Welsh Annals. There is, however, much that has been added by Geoffrey himself, apparently from his own imagination. It was, Thorpe points out, not his intention to write a record of our early history, as a chronicler would do. He set about glorifying an image of a golden age in Britain, doing so by turning chronicle into literature.

Geoffrey wrote in an unsettled time in British history. Henry I's designated successor was Matilda, his only surviving child. She was married to Geoffrey of Anjou and lived in France, and when Henry died in 1135 his nephew Stephen took the English throne. It was into this highly uncertain situation that the History was launched, and its immediate success may reflect a national need to establish an identity. It seems clear that Geoffrey himself felt a patriotic motive. Towards the end of the work he mentions a prophecy that the British people should occupy the island again some time in the future. Geoffrey himself was in a possibly ambivalent position, since he might well have come from a Norman family but was born and brought up in Wales. At the time we have not yet

Matilda of Flanders,
Queen of England

reached the period of consistent attempts to conquer Wales, and indeed the ruling monarch was too involved with self-preservation to be ambitious in expansion. It was a moment at which the concept of Britain could be

King Stephen

reinvented, and to a large extent launching King Arthur on the world had this effect.

The Arthur whom Geoffrey launched was an appropriately hybrid figure. It would be wrong to think though that he was launching this fully formed hero into a void; in fact the time was building up an Arthur-interest (as we have seen when mentioning the work of Caradoc) which was now something of a fertile seedbed. William of Malmesbury, a monk at that abbey, had published several works in the 1120s one of which promoted the historical Arthur, as derived from Nennius. Henry of Huntingdon also drew on Nennius in his *Historia Anglorum*, 'History of the English', published about 1129, to give yet another portrait of a military leader. He refers to Arthur as a mighty warrior, in command of the army and chief among the kings of Britain, who fought against the Saxons and was the victor of the Battle of Mount Badon. In other words we are still concerned with the Arthur of Nennius and the Annals, Arthur the soldier. It is not until a few years later that the other Arthur emerges, and that addition was the fruit of the enthusiastic imagination of Geoffrey of Monmouth. Geoffrey mentions all three contemporary sources (Caradoc, William and Henry) in the note in one manuscript, already referred to. But he himself, as Thorpe says, produced an Arthur "far nearer to the fictional hero of the later Arthurian romances..."

Geoffrey deals with Arthur at great length. The hero is given a long and glorious background as the son of a great king, Uther. He inherits the throne at the age of fifteen, still in a context of conflict with the Saxons. After much action (including combating the Scots, Picts and Irish) he restores the country to its earlier independence, marries Guinevere, and expands his conquests to Ireland and Iceland. At home he establishes a court, attended by a coterie of famous knights. He sets out then to conquer the whole of Europe, starting with Norway and Gaul, and in due course, after much ceremony and admiration, the Britons even capture Rome and kill the Emperor. "If I were to describe everything," writes Geoffrey – after text on Arthur running to seventeen modern pages and with a further thirty-one still to go – "I should make this story far too long." Eventually the treachery of Mordred rounds off the tale with tragedy, and both combatants die at the 'Battle of Camblam'. We have seen how Mordred appears to have been connected with the death of Arthur since the very earliest sources. "Arthur himself, our renowned king, was mortally wounded and was carried off to the Isle of Avalon, so that his wounds might be attended to."

It is surprising to us that Geoffrey's highly fanciful romance was taken at the time, and for centuries to come, to be a true record of British history. Perhaps we have to remind ourselves how unsure of its identity Britain at the time was, a pawn in the rivalry of the lines of Normandy and Anjou. Stephen of Boulogne, who had more or less seized the throne, had the advantage of having married a descendant of the Saxon royal house, and he himself possessed considerable British territories. The British dilemma could be resolved by viewing Stephen as a native rather than as a continental king. Perhaps for reasons such as that Geoffrey's material was at once taken up by representatives of both the Norman and the Saxon cultures.

Robert Wace, on the one hand, translated Geoffrey's Latin book into Norman-French, in about 1155, adding (as all compilers have) his own touch, in this case the foundation of the Round Table. Layamon a little later translated Wace's translation into what we now know as Middle English, in the form of alliterative verse. This is of interest as the first time that Arthur had occurred in English, and he takes his place now again as an emblem of a golden age, not the pre-Saxon one which he has so far represented, but a pre-Norman one in a world of Germanic saga in its exported insular form. "Might never any man think of bliss that were greater in any country than in this; might never man know any so much joy, as was with Arthur, and with his folk here!"

This function as a symbol of nostalgia continues also to run through the Welsh material from which it originally came. Arthur's versatility is demonstrated by his reinvention on his home territory at the same time as his export into other cultures. The Mabinogion tale "The Dream of Rhonabwy", for instance, which occurs in a fourteenth century manuscript but was probably written first in about 1200, is based on the idea that post-Norman Britain is a degenerate place compared to the pre-Saxon world of Arthur, who is seen here commanding a large and wealthy army. An earlier story in the Mabinogion, *Culhwch and Olwen*, perhaps written as early as 1100 but based even then on an older version, shows Arthur presiding over a centralised power, in which he bears almost supernatural status.

It is this Welsh material which is exported to France, being the apparent inspiration for the poems of Chrétien de Troyes, who wrote in Old French in the last decades of the twelfth century. Chrétien's treatment, it is now agreed, was not a simple translation of the Welsh, though in places it is very close to it. He introduced several themes which appear to be his own invention – not least the subject of the Grail. After Chrétien the material developed a French identity fast.

Following the Norman conquest barons who now possessed territory in both Britain and France encouraged the movement of troubadours between the two, and hence of their available material. Brittany in particular had the advantage of an extra linguistic link, and subject-matter moved from Wales to France by that route. Medieval French literature had for some time been occupied with two traditions: the 'Matter of Rome', mainly expansions of the story of Troy, and the 'Matter of France', which centred on the exploits of the followers of Charlemagne. The new complex of stories connected with Arthur became, in the new Anglo-French context, the 'Matter of Britain', a term first used in the twelfth century by Jean Bodel in his *Chanson des Saisnes* ('Song of the Saxons', an epic poem about a war by Charlemange against a Saxon king). A body of work now known as the Vulgate Cycle, a five-book saga, was composed by unknown writers between the years 1215 and 1230. This large work, together with minor sources both English and French, formed the base of the definitive work on the subject by Sir Thomas Malory, who finished his amalgamated version of the whole thing, *Le Morte d'Arthur*, in 1469 or 1470, and this was printed by William Caxton in 1485. That, of course, was not the end of Arthur, since he reliably lives on in another world, the world of fantasy and romance.

Into this same fantasy-land, also from various routes and through the medium of several cultures, came the wizard **Merlin**. In his origins he in fact had another name, since the early story-tellers based their idea of a poet-prophet on the largely legendary supposedly sixth-century northern British poet and warrior Myrddin ap Morfryn. This Myrddin, whether or not he existed, attracted clearly non-factual elements from an early stage. There are also a few of what some people take to be his authentic poems, though others think they belong more probably to the heroic literature of the ninth and tenth centuries. In any case they do not tell us a lot about the man, though they throw some light onto the embryo legend. This legend has clearly affected some of the poems, and of course it had time to, since they exist now only in medieval manuscripts, the late-twelfth-century Black Book of Carmarthen, and the Red Book of Hergest of about 1400.

The three sets of poems attributed to Myrddin in the Black Book have sufficient style and content in common for us to be able to treat them as the work of one writer. They are (to us, now) obscure, full of cryptic references no longer meaningful to us, with a complaining tone bemoaning the poet's wretchedness. What connects the author mainly with the later-developed legend is the reference to the battle of Arfderydd, as a result of which he went mad, took to the woods, and lived there as a wild man. This battle ties the elusive poet to fact, since it seems likely to be that mentioned by the Welsh Annals as having taken place at Arthuret, near Carlisle, in the year 573.

What is interesting about this is the very early date of the start of the legend, since it clearly has its origins in a state of

Merlin depicted as the traditional 'wild man'

warfare in the area of the Wall in the second half of the sixth century. Two archetypes are then merged into this durable figure, the Mad Prophet and the Wild Man. So clear is Merlin's duality, in fact, that later authors separated him into two characters, Merlin Wyllt, the wild Merlin (similar to the Irish hero Suibne, who was known as Suibne Geilt, the wild Suibne) – and Merlin Emrys, from the alternative derivation of his origins in the Nennius story of Ambrosius, which we will mention shortly.

Professor A. O. H. Jarman, in his booklet *The Legend of Merlin*, summarises this phase of the prophet's development: "There can be little doubt that the legend first took definite form somewhere in southern Scotland during the post-Roman era", and it is "certain that this northern tale was brought to Wales at some time between the sixth and the ninth or tenth centuries". There had been close contact between the three northern British territories (Strathclyde, Rheged and Gododdin) which now form Lowland Scotland, and the kingdom of Gwynedd, now north Wales, ever since a significant tribe of one of these territories came south under their king Cunedda in about 400 AD to free Gwynedd from Irish invaders, in the process founding the royal line which ruled northern Wales thereafter.

If it is accepted that Merlin arose from a story about a poet-warrior who went mad at the battle of Arfderydd and lived wild in the woods uttering prophecies (which seems to be the current professional opinion) we still have to explain how the Myrddin in question changed his name. The earliest source is again the History by Geoffrey of Monmouth, who transcribed and retold a vast amount of material from the same sources as those we have. He wrote in Latin. It would have been correct (it is agreed) to transliterate Myrddin as *Merdinus*. It seems that a French medievalist and teacher of the 19th century, Gaston Paris, was the first to put forward the supposition that Geoffrey baulked at the idea of perpetuating an unfortunate piece of word-play, since 'merdinus' appears to be a diminutive of the Latin *merda*, meaning 'dung', more recognisable in the French term *merde*, which everyone of Geoffrey's time would know.

This correction, from a 'd' to an 'l', is always ascribed to Geoffrey. Yet Nikolai Tolstoy points out, in his book *The Quest for Merlin*, that "The name Merlinus is in fact recorded in an Italian document of 1128, eight years before Geoffrey issued the *Historia*", and in the Annales Cambriae (in which, we have seen, the entries may well have been composed in the years to which they refer) we read for 573: "Bellum Armterid... in quo bello Guendoleu cecidit; Merlinus insanus effectus est." Gwenddolau fell; Merlin was made insane. The earliest version of the Annals which we have is in a manuscript (known as Harleian 3859) dating from the first half of the twelfth century, so given the date of availability of Geoffrey's History, 1136, the influence could have gone either way. Perhaps the correction was first made by a monastic scribe, and picked up by Geoffrey.

The literary sources of the Merlin legend, and other

Arthurian material, are split into two groups by academics, which they classify as pre- or post- Galfridian, meaning before or after Geoffrey. Much of the post-Galfridian matter is a reworking of Geoffrey's great work, but one entirely independent witness was the cleric Gerald, known to us as Giraldus Cambrensis, Gerald of Wales, who came to Wales with Archbishop Baldwin, fund-raising for a crusade, in 1188. Gerald wrote about the journey, giving us a rare insight into the Wales of this period, and he followed this in 1194 with a 'Description of Wales'. Here, in Chapter XVI, he tells us of the Welsh belief in the reality of the Wild Man/Mad Prophet combination: "There are certain persons in Cambria, whom you will find nowhere else, called Awenddyon, or people inspired...." It was, he said, in that manner "during the existence of the kingdom of the Britons, both Merlin Caledonius and Ambrosius are said to have foretold the destruction of the nation...." He has distinguished before between the two versions of Merlin, when writing about Dinas Emrys near Beddgelert, "that is, the promontory of Ambrosius, where Merlin uttered his prophecies... There were two Merlins; the one called Ambrosius, who prophesied in the time of king Vortigern, was begotten by a demon incubus, and found at Caermardin, from which circumstance that city derived the name of Carmardin, or the city of Merlin; the other Merlin born in Scotland, was named Celidonius, from the Celidonian wood in which he prophesied..This Merlin lived in the time of king Arthur, and is said to have prophesied more fully and explicitly than the other."

There are several themes here which we can dispose of briefly, but it is worth noting that the two versions of evidently the same story seem to have associated it with different periods of the past, the time of Arthur, say the sixth century, and the time of Vortigern, some two hundred years before. Geoffrey, we shall see shortly, had the same problem. First though the connection with Carmarthen may be disposed of, since although it seems to be related, through its Welsh form, Caerfyrddin, to the original Myrddin figure, this is a linguistic mistake. The name comes from the Roman name for the town, Maridunum, in turn a Romanisation of a Welsh name meaning 'sea-fort'.

Geoffrey of Monmouth took his Merlin material from Nennius, and it is there, in *Historia Brittonum*, that we find the origin of the Dinas Emrys story. When Vortigern, High-King of Britain, was forced to flee into the Welsh mountains by a rebellion of the Saxon mercenaries, he tried to build himself a castle in the fastness of Snowdonia, but all the material he had assembled for the construction disappeared overnight. So he summoned his wise men (*magi*) to ask their advice. He had to find, they said, a child without a father, and sprinkle the stronghold with his blood.

The High King sent men throughout Britain to search for the apparently impossible. Eventually they find some boys playing football, one of whom is taunted by the others with having no father. He confirms this to the messengers, and his mother also says that she does not know how he was conceived, since she had never been with a man. Geoffrey fills out the story: his mother was a nun, his father an incubus. In any case the boy is taken to Vortigern.

When confronted with the wise men the next day the boy outperformed the wizards by explaining the real reason the castle could not be built. He said there was a lake under the foundations, and in the lake were two dragons (*vermes dracones*), a white one and a red, asleep in a cloth within two vessels. When unwrapped, the dragons would fight. The wise

Dinas Emrys, a hill near Beddgelert, the supposed site of the prophesies by the original Merlin

men knew none of this. The boy explained that the red dragon was the dragon of their people, the white one 'is the dragon of the people who have seized many peoples and countries in Britain'

> and will reach almost from sea to sea; but later our people will arise, and will valiantly throw the English people across the sea.

The king asked the boy his name. "He said 'I am called Ambrosius', that is he was shown to be Emrys the Overlord." Asked about his family he replied that his father was a Roman consul. The apparent contradiction of the story here perhaps implies a background tale, to the effect that the fatherhood of Ambrosius was supposed to be a secret. In any case the Nennius version of these events ends then, with Vortigern giving Ambrosius a large amount of his kingdom, himself retreating further north.

Geoffrey then inserts his telling of the prophecies of Merlin based on this setting at Dinas Emrys. In the process he reveals a reluctance to adopt the Nennius identification with Ambrosius. The phrase "who was also called Ambrosius" is likely to be an addition. He clearly does not want his major protagonist, Merlin, to be absorbed by the Nennius prototype, who was called Ambrosius almost inevitably since the story appears to be onomastic, designed to explain the place-name Dinas Emrys. When Geoffrey takes up his story again, after the section supposedly translating Merlin's prophecies, 'Aurelius Ambrosius' becomes king of Britain. In reality Ambrosius Aurelianus is mentioned by name by Gildas, who ascribed to him the victory of Mount Badon, and seems likely to have been a historical figure of the late fifth century. We see in the Gildas description a Romanised Briton, perhaps the man responsible for the set-back in Saxon expansion, perhaps the figurehead for a national rallying, perhaps one of the prototypes for the idea of King Arthur.

Geoffrey's difficulties with recognising the two slightly incompatible appearances of Merlin become less prominent in the translations and interpretations which followed, which produced the material in due course for the 13th-century corpus known as the Vulgate Cycle, which we have become aware of while tracing the course of progress of the figure of Arthur. The second in sequence of this group is called *L'Estoire de Merlin*, itself based on a poem by Robert de Boron, From there it is a simple line to Malory, who used these French texts as his sources, and Merlin became the wizard-figure of popular culture which he is today.

It will be no surprise, after following Arthur and Merlin from their multiple roots into a fixed merged form, to learn that the **Holy Grail** also did not start out at all as it ended up.

We think of the Grail now as a chalice, a special version of the Communion cup, with even greater spiritual overtones. It started life, however, as a sort of dish, on which food could be borne. And in the form of a distant ancestry it was a magic cauldron, the model for the witches' cauldrons of later times. This in turn reminds us of Ceridwen's cauldron, in which was brewed the concoction of wisdom or inspiration, in a story connected with the poet and prophet Taliesin. The word itself, originally *graal*, is an Old French word meaning either cup or bowl, and although it acquired this name quite early in its development it had by then been through its first transformation. Ritual connections were established early, seeds of the growth of its role in religious symbolism.

Several main characters in Celtic myth possessed a magic cauldron. Bran, in the Mabinogion tale *Branwen Daughter of Llyr*, has a cauldron which can bring the dead back to life, though he rashly gives this to the king of Ireland who eventually uses it in war against him. This seems to be the same type of cauldron possessed by the Irish god known as the Dagda, and by Manannan, the Irish sea-god who gave his name to the Isle of Man. All these traditional tales come to us through medieval manuscripts, but there can be no doubt that they have early origins.

Slightly easier to date specifically is the work of Chrétien de Troyes, since it is agreed that he wrote his *Conte du Graal* sometime between the years 1180 and 1191. This is the first time the vessel is given a name, though it is clear in Chrétien that it is 'a grail' and not at this point 'the grail'. Nor is it yet of religious, let alone explicitly Christian, connection.

There is a curious relationship between the poems of Chrétien de Troyes and two Welsh tales collected in the Mabinogion. The story of *Peredur ab Efrog*, as it is originally called, 'Peredur son of Efrawg', and Chrétien's *Perceval, le Conte du Graal* already referred to, which makes us aware that Peredur, ostensibly a simple adventure story, is in fact one of the origins of the the the tales of the Grail quest, the innocent hero, the Castle of Wonders. Several images arise in Peredur, in fact, which become major symbols in later works, such as the castle by the river and the Fisher King.

There are enough similarities between the Chrétien poem and Peredur to make it clear that they have at least a common root. There are enough differences between them to show that neither is simply a translation of the other. It would probably be possible, by textual analysis, to show how far they have come from their common original, and so to work out the real age of the material. Indeed, in the vast academic literature on the subject, this has probably already been done. Though the workmanship of 'Peredur' appears to date from about 1250, and so to be later than *Perceval*, the material has an older aspect to it, a feeling of the excavation of ancient mysteries.

Peredur was the youngest of seven sons of an earl, Efrawg. His father and brothers were killed in combat, but he, being too young to go to war, survived. In due course he sets off for Arthur's court, and after some adventures there he goes on his way further, into and beyond a forest. He comes to a castle by a lake, where an elderly man sits fishing, who, when he gets up to go back in, turns out to be lame. These early references to the ailing fisher king who can be saved by the

93

grail are not developed here, but seem as inexplicable to the story-teller as they are to his protagonist.

He comes to what appears to us to be a clear prototype of the Castle of Wonders, where more unexplained events and tests take place. His host (his uncle, as it turns out) converses with him over dinner, while highly ritualistic things take place. Two youths pass through the great hall carrying a spear, from which flow three streams of blood. This causes much lamentation among the diners. After a pause two maidens enter, "and a great salver between them, and a man's head on the salver, and blood in profusion around the head." *Dysgl*, meaning a dish or cup, but in this case clearly a receptacle big enough to bear a severed head.

> Dyma ddwy forwyn yn dyfod a dysgl fawr rhyngddynt, a phen gwr ar y ddysgl, a gwaed lawer o'i gylch.

He does not ask what is the meaning of all this, having been warned not to ask questions. However (before we think of taking this advice ourselves) the story admits a contradiction, since he is later told that if he had asked the crucial questions – what was the meaning or cause of the marvels he saw, the spear running with streams of blood, and the maidens bearing the severed head on a platter – had he asked about them the king would have regained his health and his kingdom would have been restored to peace.

Chrétien does not offer the severed head, but in its place on the platter (*graal*) is a single communion wafer, and the crucial question is: whom does it serve? It emerges that it sustains the Fisher King's maimed father, who would have been healed had the hero asked the question. This is the first intimation of a connection with the sacrament, and it meshes well with the grail's other ancestry, the Cauldron of Rebirth.

It is Robert de Boron who introduces to the story the larger and seemingly separate theme of the holy chalice's connection with the Last Supper and the blood of Christ. De Boron was a Burgundian from near the modern Swiss border. In his poem *Joseph d'Arimathie* (which he wrote sometime between 1191 and 1202) he names the Fisher King as Bron, and firmly identifies the graal as a chalice (*calice*).

How Joseph of Arimathea became involved in all this is intriguing, and its consequences were considerable, since it not only linked the Holy Grail with the Last Supper and the Crucifixion but brought it to Britain and more specifically to Glastonbury. R. S. Loomis, in his book *The Gail, from Celtic Myth to Christian Symbol*, traces the origin of the elaboration of this to texts in the Apochrypha which supplied ideas incorporated in the first member of the Vulgate cycle, *L'Estoire del Saint Graal*, which was in effect a prose version of de Boron's poem. The complications of additions to the twelfth century French literature are considerable, but the result of them is that by the beginning of the 13th century the grail is characterised as the cup which Christ raised at the Last Supper, which was then acquired by Joseph of Arimathea and used by him to collect the blood still flowing from Christ's body after the Crucifixion. At a later period, in Germany, it became a stone, (the 'lapis exilis' which had come from the Garden of Eden), yet still possessing the established grail properties of discriminating and providing abundance. Wolfram von Eschenbach drew from Chrétien's poem, in the early years of the thirteenth century, a long poem which he called after its hero 'Parzival', which has been greatly influential, largely due to its later influence on Wagner. It was however the use made by Malory of the

The ruins of Glastonbury Abbey, long connected with the Holy Grail

French material in the Vulgate Cycle which propelled the matter forward towards our current understanding: Tennyson and the Romantics, the pre-Raphaelite painters, modern films and fictional books.

It remains to be explained how and why the idea of the Grail came to Glastonbury. It was mentioned by Robert de Boron that the Grail-bearers were going to a distant westward land, which was referred to more specifically as the 'Vaus d'Avaron'. Avalon was the name of a Celtic otherworld which became identified at a certain time with Glastonbury. This link is reinforced by another version of the story, a French prose work known as 'Perlesvaus', written probably sometime between 1191 and 1225. That text refers to Arthur's burial at Avalon, and towards the end of the work what is evidently Glastonbury is mentioned again, with a description of the Tor (*la montaigne de la valee*). But that is all we have to go on, in the way of textual support. It was the Abbey records themselves, subject of course to the loyalty of their scribes, which set the train in motion. Glastonbury abbey was founded by the disciples of Christ. Somebody at some point in the early thirteenth century added the information that one of these disciples was Joseph of Arimathea, and about a

Glastonbury Tor

hundred years later it was taken as established fact that Joseph founded Glastonbury, bringing with him (in the Abbey version) two cruets, perhaps preferred by the monks as having less of a pagan air about them than a drinking vessel, containing the blood and sweat of Christ.

R. S. Loomis, who has done a great deal of work on this subject, suggests that Joseph of Arimathea became involved in the whole matter by mistake. The sacred vessel, in his theory, was originally a magic drinking horn, such as that horn of plenty said to belong to Bran in some of the Welsh tradition. Loomis's argument is that 'cors benoit', meaning sacred horn, could also mean 'holy body', the body of Christ, and it was Joseph who owned that.

Williiam of Malmesbury, twelfth-century historian, acted as a sort of publicity officer for the great Abbey in about 1125 and made the story into official history, which, Loomis points out, has led people to believe that the early history of the Grail was no more than "a piece of Glastonbury propaganda, deliberately fabcricated to enhance the prestige and increase the revenues of the holy house" .

There is, on the face of it, nothing surprising about that. We have encountered throughout this investigation the benefits of not letting the facts get in the way of a good story.

Bibliography

ARTHUR:

Nennius, *British History and the Welsh Annals*, ed. & trs. John Morris, Phillimore, London, 1980.

Gildas, *The Ruin of Britain and other documents*, ed. & trs. Michael Winterbottom, Phillimore, London, 1978.

N. J. Higham, *The English Conquest*, Manchester University Press, 1994.

Geoffrey Ashe, *From Caesar to Arthur*, Collins, London, 1960.

Aneirin, *Y Gododdin*, ed, A. O. H. Jarman, Gomer Press, 1988.

Gwyn Williams, ed. & trs. *The Burning Tree*, Faber, London, 1956.

Geoffrey of Monmouth, *The History of the Kings of Britain*, ed. & trs. Lewis Thorpe, Penguin, 1966.

MERLIN:

Welsh Annals, as above.

A. O. H. Jarman, *The Legend of Merlin*, University of Wales Press, 1976.

Giraldus Cambrensis, *The Itinerary through Wales* and *Description of Wales*, Dent, Everyman, 1935.

Nikolai Tolstoy, *The Quest for Merlin*, Hamish Hamilton, London, 1985.

Gwyn Williams, *An Introduction to Welsh Poetry*, Faber, London, 1953.

Geoffrey of Monmouth, as above.

THE GRAIL

The Mabinogion, ed. & trs. Gwyn Jones and Thomas Jones, Dent, Everyman, 1957.

R. S. Loomis, *The Grail, from Celtic Myth to Christian Symbol*, University of Wales Press, 1963.

The Quest of the Holy Grail, ed. & trs. P. M. Matarosso, Penguin, 1969.

Other books by the same author

Visit our website for further information:
www.carreg-gwalch.com

Orders can be placed on our
On-line Shop

Heritage

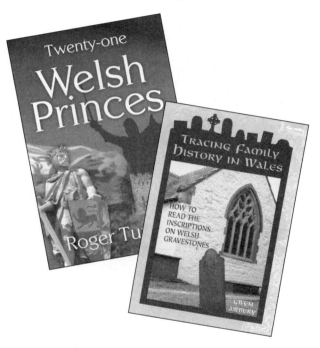

Visit our website for further information:
www.carreg-gwalch.com

Orders can be placed on our
On-line Shop

Welsh Churches and their Heritage

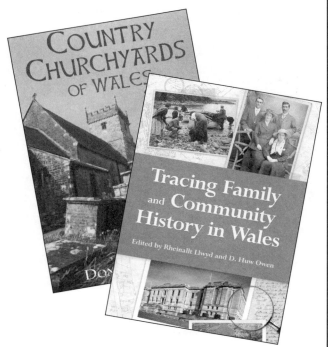

Visit our website for further information:
www.carreg-gwalch.com

Orders can be placed on our
On-line Shop

Further enjoyable reading on History and Heritage

Visit our website for further information:
www.carreg-gwalch.com

Orders can be placed on our
On-line Shop